The Large Amphibian Groups

This scheme does not follow the classification criteria used today. Its only aim is to indicate the different paths of evolutionary development the individual orders followed, regardless of their origins or kinship. The dotted line indicates only a hypothetical link, since the fossils of the animals that gave rise to both modern and extinct amphibians are still inadequate and incomplete.

Anurans

toward the Reptiles

Stereospondyli

Seymouriamorphs

Rhachitomi

Embolomeri

THE HISTORY OF LIFE ON EARTH

AMPHIBIANS

© 1987 English-language edition by Facts On File, Inc.
460 Park Avenue South, New York, NY 10016

© 1987 Editoriale Jaca Book Spa, Milano

editorial coordination
CATERINA LONGANESI

CONTENTS

1. In the Waters of the Devonian Period
2. The Sarcopterygians
3. The *Latimeria*
4. Extinct and Living Dipnoans
5. Living Dipnoans
6. The Preadaptation of Rhipidistians
7. The Stage Amphibians Appeared On
8. What Makes an Amphibian: The Skeleton
9. What Makes an Amphibian: The Ear and the Eye
10. The First Amphibians Appear: The *Ichthyostega*
11. The Era of the Amphibians
12. Longer Bodies
13. The Origin of Living Amphibians
14. The Features of Amphibians: Metamorphosis
15. Mating and Parental Care
16. Respiration, Voice, and Blood
17. How They Feed
18. How They Move
19. The Skin and Hibernation
20. Apodes
21. Urodeles
22. Salamanders and Newts
23. Anurans
24. True Toads
25. Frogs
26. The Frog's Natural Enemies and Camouflage
27. The Decline of Ancient Amphibians
28. Amphibians Become Similar to Reptiles

Library of Congress Cataloging-in-Publication Data

Minelli, Giuseppe.
  Amphibians.

  (History of life on earth)
  Translation and adaptation of: Gli anfibi.
  Summary: Describes the physical characteristics of amphibians and traces their evolutionary history on earth.
    1. Amphibians—Evolution—Juvenile literature.
2. Amphibians, Fossil—Juvenile literature.
[1. Amphibians. 2. Amphibians, Fossil] I. Minelli, G. Anfibi. English. II. Berselli R. - Tamer M. ill. III. Title. IV. Series.
QL667.M5613 1987   597.6   86-32907.
ISBN 0-8160-1557-0

color separation by
Carlo Scotti, Milano
photosetting by
Elle Due, Milano
printed and bound in Italy by
Tipolitografia G. Canale & C. Spa, Torino

AMPHIBIANS

Giuseppe Minelli

Professor of Comparative Anatomy
University of Bologna, Italy

illustrated by
Remo Berselli and Marzio Tamer

translated by
Bryan Fleming

the "History of Life on Earth" series
is conceived, designed and produced by
Jaca Book

Facts On File Publications
New York, New York ● Oxford, England

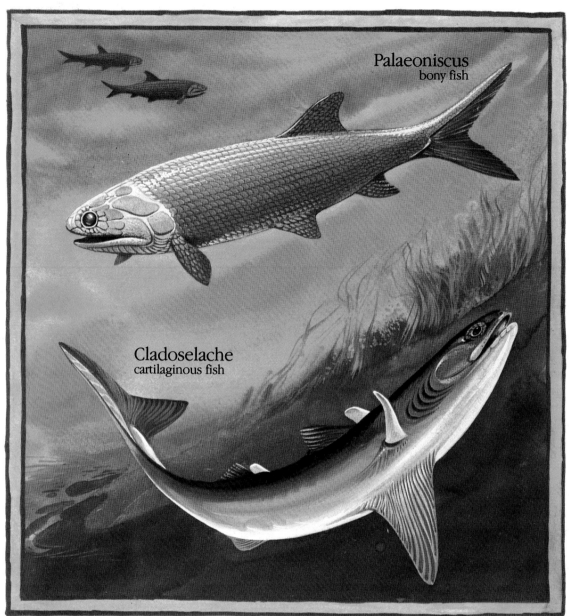

Fish with cartilaginous skeletons and the first specimens of bony fish dominated the seas of the Devonian Period. They lived in cold, clear waters rich in oxygen.

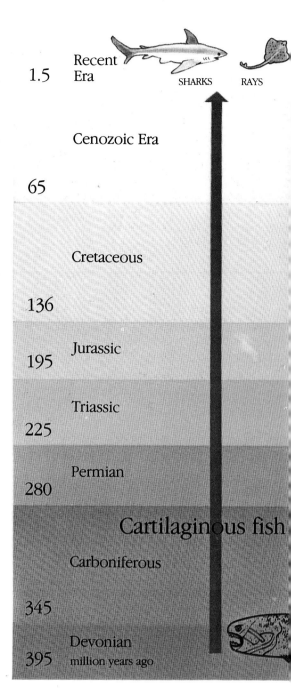

1.5 Recent Era

SHARKS   RAYS

Cenozoic Era

65

Cretaceous

136

Jurassic
195

Triassic

225

Permian
280

Cartilaginous fish

Carboniferous

345

Devonian
395 million years ago

The main evolutionary lines of modern fish.

1. IN THE WATERS OF THE DEVONIAN PERIOD

In the waters of the Devonian Period, from 345 to 400 million years ago, the evolution of fish was taking place. The ancient groups, such as the ostracoderms and the placoderms, were about to disappear, while two great evolutionary lines were developing in different environments.

In the saltwater seas, the first bony fish were beginning to make their presence felt; fish with cartilaginous skeletons were becoming widespread. As we can read in the *Marine Life* volume in this series, the cartilaginous fish gave rise to our present-day sharks and rays. Meanwhile, in the brackish or fresh waters, a different kind of fish with a bony skeleton was flourishing. Its different marine environment caused it to become differentiated very early on.

THE LAND IN THE DEVONIAN PERIOD

The environment of the land above sea level in the Devonian Period was probably very boring. Wetlands, with shallow, warm water prevailed. Mountains with running streams and cold waters were relatively rare. Out of the water, the first plants with tall stems, such as ferns and horestails, were appearing, and the first woods, inhabited by the first invertebrates—which had left the water—were on the point of developing. This environment, with shallow, warm water, did not suit the typical anatomical organization of fish. It was difficult for them to swim, and more importantly, their gills could not take in enough oxygen from the water to meet their needs.

THE OXYGEN IN THE WATER

According to a law of physics, the colder the water, the more gas it contains. Conversely, only a small amount of gas can be dissolved in warm water. Oxygen—a fundamental element for animal life—is a gas, and therefore follows this law. In a warm environment with stagnant waters, neither atmospheric oxygen nor the oxygen produced by water plants can dissolve.

2

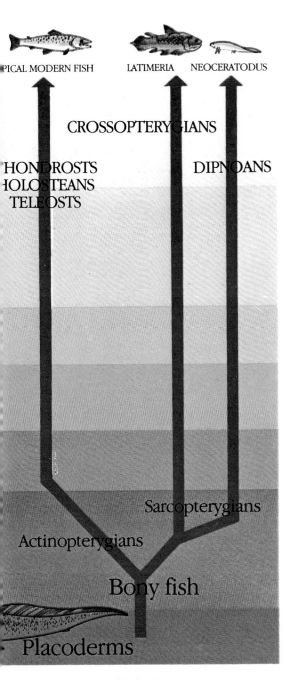

CROSSOPTERYGIANS

CHONDROSTS
HOLOSTEANS
TELEOSTS

DIPNOANS

PICAL MODERN FISH   LATIMERIA   NEOCERATODUS

Sarcopterygians

Actinopterygians

Bony fish

Placoderms

Eusthenopteron
crossopterygian

Dipterus
dipnoan

The lack of oxygen in the warm and shallow fresh water of the wetlands in the Devonian Period favored the development of bony fish, the sarcopterygians, which were able to breathe air, too, through a rudimentary lung.

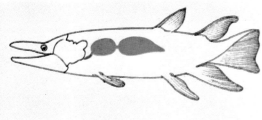

THE AIR BLADDER

The primitive lung used by sarcopterygians to breathe in oxygen from the atmosphere is traditionally called an air bladder, or swim bladder, even though it is not used at all for swimming. This misnomer stems from the fact that the bladder was seen for the first time in teleosts—the most typical bony fish—in which it does perform the function after which it is named. (The air bladder or swim bladder is discussed in the *Marine Life* volume in this series.) Only later was it discovered that some fish, such as the dipnoans, used this bladder as a lung, but the name was already in everyday language, and still is today.

Oxygen produced by plants through photosynthesis tends to surface in the form of small bubbles. So these plants—like all others, great producers of oxygen, as we all know—cannot provide the warm, shallow, stagnant waters with sufficient oxygen. It is practically impossible for fish to live in such an environment, unless they find a new way of oxygenating their blood.

BREATHING AIR

Breathing air was, perhaps, not a totally new thing; maybe some of the ancient placoderms had already developed a diverticulum, an extension of the intestine, in the form of a little pulmonary sac with respiratory functions. Fossil imprints tell us this may well have happened. The diverticulum definitely appeared in a primitive group of bony fish, and was a successful means of colonizing the fresh waters of the Devonian Period. These fish learned to breathe both with their gills and with that sort of primitive lung which we now wrongly call an air bladder.

THE NOSTRILS AND THE CHOANAS

However, there had to be some new duct to take oxygen to the lung, primitive as it was. Up to then, fish had used their olfactory pits only for perceiving smells in the water. Closed at the end, the pits communicated with the outside environment solely by means of the same opening through which water came in and went out. Now, they turned into real nostrils, and performed two tasks: they perceived smells, and let air pass through. Besides communicating with the outer environment, they opened into the inner wall of the mouth, with two ducts and two holes called *choanas*. The oxygen entering nostrils could pass into the mouth by means of the choanas, and then reach the lung. Fish with nostrils and choanas are called choanichthyes, or more commonly, sarcopterygians—or *Sarcopterygii*—and they can also breathe the oxygen in the air. These were the new bony fish that appeared in the warm, shallow, brackish or fresh waters of the Devonian Period.

3

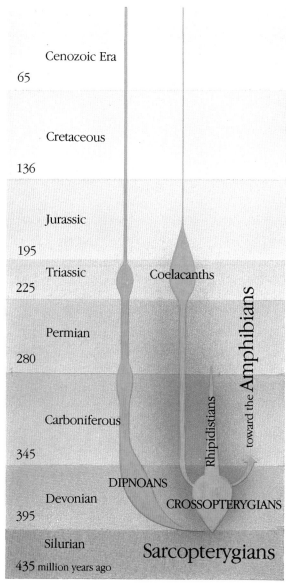

Cenozoic Era	
65	
Cretaceous	
136	
Jurassic	
195	
Triassic	Coelacanths
225	
Permian	
280	
Carboniferous	
345	
	DIPNOANS
Devonian	CROSSOPTERYGIANS
395	
Silurian	Sarcopterygians
435 million years ago	

Rhipidistians · toward the Amphibians

The main evolutionary lines of sarcopterygian fish.

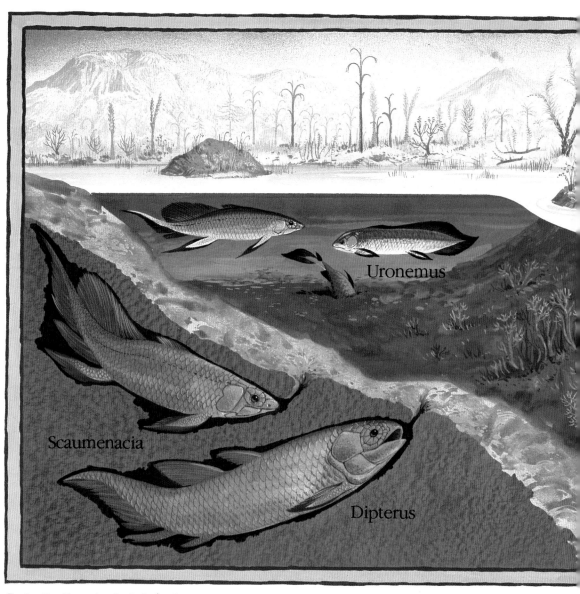

Uronemus · Scaumenacia · Dipterus

During the Devonian Period, the dipnoans, which lived in the fresh or brackish waters of the wetlands, solved the problem of surviving in drought periods by sinking into the muddly depths, where they stayed as though in hibernation, waiting for better times to come.

2. THE SARCOPTERYGIANS
(Dipnoans, Coelacanths, Rhipidistians)

As we have seen, in the warm, shallow waters of the Devonian Period, about 400 million years ago, there appeared the sarcopterygians—the first fish that could breathe air through a rudimental lung. In that kind of water, poor in oxygen, the new development was soon rewarded by evolution. The sarcopterygians met instant success, and it did not take them long to colonize that environment where, for a long time, they remained the only vertebrates. The other, cartilaginous and bony fish, in fact, could only breathe through their gills, so they could not survive in the hostile waters. The sarcopterygians—the word means "fleshy-finned fish"—having no direct competitors, spread rapidly, and gave rise to two different species of fish: *Dipnoi* and *Crossopterygii*—we shall call them dipnoans and crossopterygians—which had solved the problem of survival in shallow, warm waters in a different way.

DIPNOANS

While consolidating the innovation of breathing air, these sarcopterygians (which we shall examine more closely in Chapters 4 and 5) retained certain old features, such as a bony skull cover. But to live in a warm, swampy environment, where a long drought might dry up the water resources, it was necessary to solve a great problem: how to survive during unfavorable periods. The solution adopted by dipnoans—which means "with two breathing systems"—that still live on today, and perhaps also by those that thrived in the Devonian Period, was to sink into the mud in the form of a cocoon covered with a hardened secretion. The cocoon was open only near the mouth, so that the fish could breathe the air they needed to survive. This choice affected the skeletal structure of their fins, as we shall see in Chapter 4, and this actually prevented the dipnoans from being the protagonists of the transition from water to dry land.

CROSSOPTERYGIANS

This second group of fish was more successful and widespread in all the fresh waters of the Devonian Period; indeed, the evolutionary strength of its members led some of them to venture into the seas, where they had to face competition from the first bony and cartilaginous fish. But freshwater crossopterygians —the word means "lobe-finned fish"—are more essential to the plot of our story. They discovered another solution to the problem of an environment that was drying up. Rather than sink into the slime and somehow manage to survive, they sought deeper waters to live and reproduce in. But this required a different skeleton than that of a typical fish. The architecture of the spine, and especially of the fin skeleton, had to change in order to enable the fish to move about on dry land, even though when they eventually did it was in an awkward, goofy manner. The crossopterygians who took on this way of life are included in the suborder of *Rhipidistia*—the rhipidistians—and vertebrates able to leave the water, and adapt to life on dry land and to breathing air will appear among them. One of the rhipidistians that was organized similarly to the most primitive amphibians is *Eusthenopteron*—even though we consider it more a witness, rather than the protagonist, of the transition from one class to another. This fish could already move on dry land, as we can tell from the shape of

Holoptychius

Eusthenopteron

Fossil of *Eusthenopteron*, a rhipidistian crossopterygian of the Devonian Period, regarded as an ancestor of the amphibians.

In that same Period, the rhipidistian crossopterygians learned how to crawl out of the ponds that were drying up, and go off in search of deeper water. Thus was created the basis for a very important event in the history of evolution: vertebrates left the water and took possession of dry land.

THE INFLUENCE OF THE ENVIRONMENT

The history of the sarcopterygians is extremely important for an understanding of relations between the anatomical organization of a creature and its environment. No amphibian arises from the typical organization of fish. On the contrary; the possibility of colonizing swamps with warm, shallow waters lacking oxygen gave rise to a completely different kind of fish, not so different in shape as in functions and skeletal structure.

All this is possible only if evolution has enough time—score after score of millions of years—and constant temperature and humidity levels, and so on. In this case, the environment is productive. But if excessively sudden changes take place, then it becomes destructive: species have insufficient time to cope with the new adaptation, and are inexorably condemned to extinction, which is exactly what happened to the rhipidistians at the beginning of the Permian Period.

the skeleton and fin. The structure of its teeth is also similar to that of primitive amphibians (see Chapter 10).

THE IMPORTANCE OF THE RHIPIDISTIANS

At a certain moment, paleontologists, by examining the features of the various fish, came to the conclusion that only the crossopterygians could have had the anatomical and functional characteristics needed for them to leave the water. More particularly, only the rhipidistians among them could have been the protagonists of this exceptionally important event. Thus, greater scientific attention was paid to these animals, and the result has been a series of detailed studies on their skeletons. Unfortunately, all of these fish are extinct. Nevertheless, comparisons with the oldest known amphibians abound. One aim is to discover the identity of the leading star, or stars, that broke the barrier which separated aquatic life and terrestrial life.

THE EXTINCTION OF THE RHIPIDISTIANS

This important crossopterygian group did not manage to survive through the Carboniferous Period. When the warm, humid environmental conditions of the Carboniferous Period became, in the Permian Period, cold and dry first, and then warm and dry, the situation became impossible for the ill-fated rhipidistians. In those environments, owing either to the cold and the ice crust that prevented fish from coming up to the surface to breathe, or to the torrid climate, where most of the waters were drying up—and there seemed to be no sense in migrating in search of a more favorable climate—the rhipidistians were inexorably sentenced to death. Not one of them survived the Permian Period; 280 million years ago, all had disappeared. Today, all that is left to us of this basic group of fish is a little fossil evidence, skeletons or tooth prints, and nothing else. It is a great pity. If some of them had survived, we would know so much more about how the transition from fish to amphibians occurred! But we do know something about it.

Macroponia

Latimeria

In the Devonian Period, some crossopterygians, the coelacanths, left the fresh water to invade the sea.

Inset: the few specimens of *Latimeria* which have been caught have been carefully studied to help us understand one of the creatures that began the transition from fish to amphibian.

3. THE LATIMERIA
(Coelacanths)

THE ORIGINS OF *LATIMERIA*: COELACANTHS

In the previous chapter, we have briefly seen that not all the crossopterygians were content with colonizing the warm brackish or fresh waters in lagoons or swamps. In the second half of the Devonian Period, a small group of crossopterygians, coelacanths—such as *Latimeria* and *Macroponia*—ventured into the cold, deep waters of the seas. They owe their survival to this decision. While the original group, the rhipidistians, died out because they found living conditions in the fresh waters of the Permian Period impossible, the coelacanths went on living in the cold, quiet, deep seawaters until the middle of the Jurassic Period. Then, they too became extinct, or at least it was believed so since there was no fossil evidence from that period on.

But in 1938-39, an exciting piece of news astonished the world of science: a coelacanth had been discovered, and it was still alive and kicking!

LATIMERIA REDISCOVERED

The story of how this important fish was lost and found again deserves special mention, as it is a fine example of how scientific discoveries can occur.

At East London, a small port on the South African coast, there was a very modest natural history museum run by Mrs. Courtenay-Latimer (note the second surname!), who was sometimes offered unusual, unmarketable fish from the local fishermen. At the end of December 1938, they brought a large fish, over 5 feet (1.5 meters) long, to Mrs. Latimer's small laboratory. The lady had never seen one of them before, and did not know how to classify it. In her uncertainty, she made a sketch of the creature, along with a few notes about certain peculiarities she thought might be important: "the fins look vaguely like limbs, and they have scales up to the point where they spread out." The sketch and notes were sent to Professor J.L.B. Smith of the Grahamstone University, South Africa. Smith immediately understood, with great excitement, how exceptional the discovery was: in the rough sketch and brief description, he had recognized the features of a crossopterygian, the specimen of a fish group thought to have become extinct millions of years before. The professor immediately sent a telegram to Mrs. Latimer telling her how important the find was, and begging her to conserve the specimen in the very best way possible.

But it was too late; too much time had passed, and the animal had been stuffed. Only the skin and the skeleton had been preserved, while all the precious inner parts were lost forever. Nevertheless, in 1939, Professor Smith announced to the scientific world the discovery of the new fish, which he called *Latimeria* in honor of the good lady, and *Chalumnae*, to commemorate the place where it had been fished, at the mouth of the river Chalumna.

THE REWARD

After having recognized the exceptional animal, Professor Smith devoted all his efforts to the search for another specimen, which he ardently wished to examine carefully, the soft parts in particular. Partly because of the Second World War, and partly owing to the difficulty of getting funds, all the efforts the professor made were in vain. In 1948, he even printed some leaflets bearing a picture of a stuffed *Latimeria* promising a reward of £ 100 to the person who caught, preserved, and sent him another. But time passed, and nobody showed up to collect the reward. Only in December 1952, 14 years after the first

A *Latimeria* being caught in a small harbor at East London, South Africa, in 1938. Left: today, this living fossil may only be photographed in its environment.

In 1948 some leaflets were printed with a picture of *Latimeria*, promising a reward of £ 100 to the person who caught another, dead or alive.

LATIMERIA TODAY

So far, fewer than thirty *Latimeria* have been fished, but unlike a few years ago, the animal is now strictly protected. If it is caught, it must be thrown back into the water. Only a few authorized people are empowered to organize special fishing expeditions in the waters inhabited by *Latimeria*. Today, thankfully, all one is allowed to do is take pictures of it, or study it in its natural environment without disturbing it. The research of the French ichthyologists, however, have provided us with the most interesting data, so that we now know the fish fairly well. One important fact is the regression of the creature's air bladder, which was used by the rhipidistian's ancestors to take advantage of the oxygen in the atmosphere. As the oxygen dissolved in seawater is good enough for the needs of *Latimeria*, their ability to breathe air disappeared, while the air bladder—their former primitive lung—turned into a capacious ball of fat, maybe to lower their specific weight. The *Latimeria* today is 5 feet (1.5 meters) long, and has an enormous mouth armed with sharp teeth. Its body is covered by strong, dark blue scales that reach out as far as its stumpy, paired pectoral fins. Its tail, just as stumpy, is typical of the species.

specimen was found, did a telegram finally arrive. It was from the Comoro Archipelago, off the coast of Madagascar, and announced that a second specimen had been caught. Professor Smith took the first plane, and rushed to the place, where he was lucky enough to be the first to study the general anatomy of the *Latimeria*. Madagascar was then a French possession, and from that moment on, most of the research on the *Latimeria* was carried out by French experts.

SCIENCE AND FISHERMEN

In the forties and fifties, scientists were bending over backward in their endeavor to find specimens of *Latimeria*, while the fishermen of the Comoro Islands and Madagascar had always been quite familiar with the creature.

Indeed, when they caught one of them, the fishermen first cursed the uneatable fish—for it is said to have a revolting taste—and promptly proceeded to skin the animal, use its skin as sandpaper, and threw the rest into the sea!

Who knows? The sea might well have other surprises in store for us. And somewhere, someone—without knowing it—may long since have made a discovery that will shake the world of science when it becomes known.

Dipterus

Scaumenacia

Sarcopterygian fins. Left: the heavy, stumpy pectoral fin of a rhipidistian (*Eusthenopteron*). Right: the slender, threadlike fin of a dipnoan (African lungfish).

Two extinct dipnoans: *Dipterus* is the most ancient known one; *Scaumenacia* is the most recent.

Right-hand page: the Australian lungfish is in danger of extinction because of its inability to leave rivers that dry up

4. EXTINCT AND LIVING DIPNOANS
(Ceratodidae)

This order of sarcopterygians long inhabited the Earth's fresh waters in the Devonian and Triassic Period, from about 400 to 195 million years ago. These creatures lived in rivers, swamps, and marshes together with other sarcopterygians and rhipidistians, who not only took in oxygen contained in water, but were also able to use oxygen in the air. In Chapter 2, we have already seen that these two groups of fish found a different way of solving the problem of survival when heat and the absence of rainfall caused a shortage of water. The rhipidistians had learnt to leave the water and crawl on the ground using their stumpy fins to propel themselves towards deeper pools. The dipnoans, instead, stayed where they were, burrowed in the mud. This different behavior caused changes to take place in the skeletons of the two kinds of sarcopterygians.

THE EVOLUTION OF FINS

In rhipidistians, evolution favored strong fins with articulated bones, which enabled the fish to take short walks on the land. In dipnoans, which never left the water, the fins became thinner, and sometimes turned into threadlike organs. The creatures used them in the same way, however, because even very thin fins help the fish to move on the seabed. Walking under the water was much easier because the weight of the body was not sustained by the fins, but by the water itself, thanks to the famous Archimedes' law (see the *Marine Life* volume in this series).

Their different life-styles and the different skeletal structure of their fins sent the two groups of fish off towards different destinies. When favorable conditions ceased, almost all the dipnoans disappeared, save three, which are still with us today, while the rhipidistians died out completely.

THE DISTRIBUTION OF DIPNOANS

The oldest dipnoan we know is the *Dipterus*, which was thriving as early as the Devonian Period. About a foot (30 centimeters) long, it is classified as a dipnoan, both because of the communication between its olfactory pits and mouth, which it needed in order to breathe air, and of the skeletal structure of its fins. From this period on, dipnoans were to be found in all the Earth's fresh water, though not in large numbers. This widespread distribution can only be explained by the continental drift, the phenomenon that took place in the Devonian Period, when the land above sea level—one single block—broke up to form the continents we have today. Dipnoans, in fact, definitely could not migrate into the seas, which also explains the current location of the survivors: Australia, Africa and South America—tropical areas, where rivers and lakes tend to dry up easily.

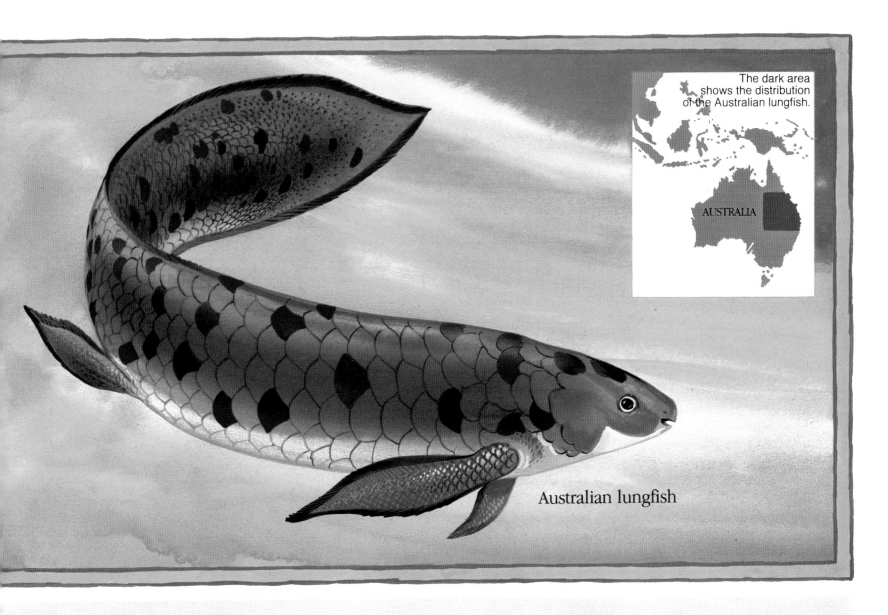

The dark area shows the distribution of the Australian lungfish.

AUSTRALIA

Australian lungfish

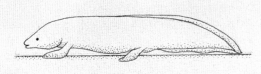 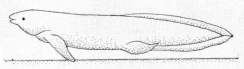 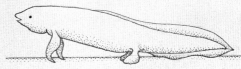

The fins of the Australian lungfish, like those of the other dipnoans, are not really suitable for swimming, but they are very useful for moving on the river beds.

LIVING DIPNOANS

Dipnoans have been known officially by science for more than two centuries, but their anatomy and their ability to breathe by means of one lung have only recently been the subject of exhaustive study. They did not make headlines in the clamorous way the *Latimeria* did when they were discovered. But these gaunt specimens of a great and glorious group of fish have slowly but surely attracted everyone's interest. They have even acquired common names—besides the official scientific ones—such as "lungfish" in English, and "Lurchfische" (frog fish) in German. Three classes only have survived, each living in its own corner of the world.

THE AUSTRALIAN LUNGFISH

This is the only survivor of the *Ceratodus* family, which was distributed over all the Earth's surface in the Triassic Period. The Australian lungfish, *Neoceratodus forsteri*, can be more than 3 feet (1 meter) long, and can weigh over 22 pounds (10 kilos). What makes it different from the other two classes are its stumpy, heavy fins and its single lung. Its meat, unfortunately, is excellent, so it is already rare, the result of being overfished, and is running the risk of becoming extinct. Nowadays, it can be found in the waters of Queensland, where it is protected by law. Endeavors have also been made to have it migrate to deeper waters, such as the small lakes of this region. The way the Australian lungfish manages to survive in dry periods shows how primitive it is. The other living dipnoans (Chapter 5) can burrow down into the mud and keep alive even though the river dries up completely. The Australian lungfish, on the other hand, takes refuge in the last remaining puddles, and stays there motionless, breathing the oxygen in the air. In this situation, it runs two risks, it can easily be caught by man or predators; or can die, if the puddle dries up. The threat of its extinction could probably be countered by somehow moving the creature permanently to areas that are unlikely to dry up. It would be a great pity if we lost the Australian lungfish, for it opens an important chapter in the history of vertebrates.

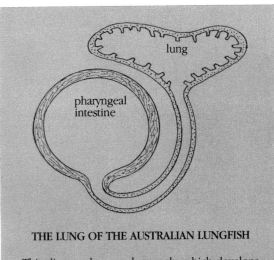

THE LUNG OF THE AUSTRALIAN LUNGFISH

This dipnoan has one lung only, which develops from the ventral part of the pharingeal intestine. The inner walls are highly vascularized, and have little folds to make breathing easier. This lung can only provide enough oxygen for survival. When the Australian lungfish is active, it has to breathe with its gills as well.

SOUTH AMERICA

The dark area shows the distribution of South American lungfish.

The South American lungfish lives in the rivers of the equatorial forests and, in case of necessity, it can dig a burrow in the muddy depths, where it stays until water accumulates again.

South American lungfish

5. LIVING DIPNOANS
(*Lepidosirenidae*)

The South American and the African lungfish are the most evolved dipnoans, with thin, slender fins and only one lung, which develops from a ventral diverticulum in the first part of the pharyngeal intestine, just as in amphibians. Both are able to survive even in lakes or rivers that have completely dried up because they burrow in the mud, where they can live while waiting for the water to return.

THE SOUTH AMERICAN LUNGFISH

Before the first South American lungfish was found, nobody really knew how great the development of sarcopterygians had been in ancient eras, and this fish, with two working lungs, truly caused amazement. Indeed, the scientists were so astonished that they called it *Lepidosiren paradoxa*, which underlines the fact that the animal has illogical features. Today, we know that it is not paradoxical at all, and it is classified in the sarcopterygian group on account of its features. This lungfish, which is up to 3 feet (1 meter) long, inhabits certain South American basins, especially the Amazon and all its tributaries. Thanks to the broad extension of these areas—which are rich in water,

thinly populated, and free of pollution—it is believed that this dipnoan is not likely to become extinct.

THE AFRICAN LUNGFISH

The African lungfish, *Protopterus*, is the dipnoan that has received the most attention. It can live in captivity, and when it has burrowed deep down into a block of clay, it can be taken from one place to another without suffering. It is to be seen in the better zoos worldwide. Its body is as slender as that of the South American lungfish, so it can dig excellent burrows, in which it lives, even when there is no drought. For instance, during the mating season, the male fish digs a large tunnel, and then leads the female—or females, rather—into it. After spawning, the female does not look after the eggs while they develop; it is the male that takes care of them, keeps them clean, drives off any predator, and protects the larvae, which hatch, and have to go through metamorphosis before becoming independent. Both the African and the South American lungfish have a very unusual way of developing for fish: they metamorphose.

The lungs of the South American and African lungfish are double, and develop from the ventral diverticulum of the pharyngeal intestine.

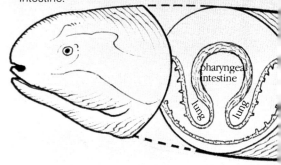

pharyngeal intestine

lung

lung

10

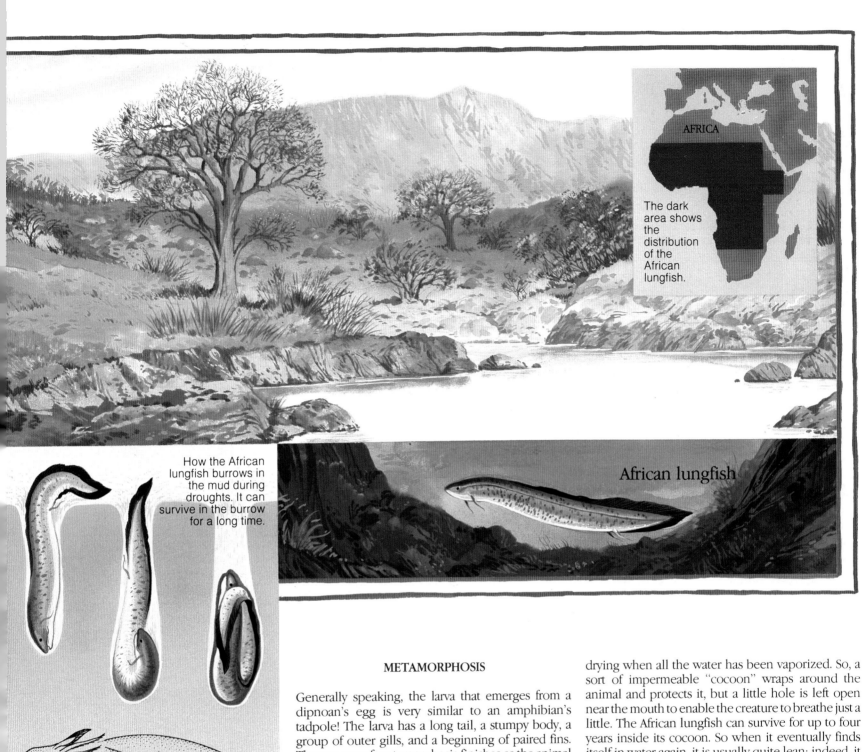

The dark area shows the distribution of the African lungfish.

AFRICA

African lungfish

How the African lungfish burrows in the mud during droughts. It can survive in the burrow for a long time.

Larva of the African lungfish.

Opened block of hardened mud with a living African lungfish.

METAMORPHOSIS

Generally speaking, the larva that emerges from a dipnoan's egg is very similar to an amphibian's tadpole! The larva has a long tail, a stumpy body, a group of outer gills, and a beginning of paired fins. The process of metamorphosis finishes as the animal develops: its body lengthens, its outer gills disappear, and the creature acquires all the features of the adult. In the African lungfish, subsequent development is extremely fast: in only three months, a fish 2 inches (5 centimeters) long grows to a foot (about 35 centimeters) in length. It probably grows so rapidly because it needs to attain the right size and strength to dig burrows in the mud and keep safe when the hot season comes. This fish lives in streams that regularly dry up in August and December, so by that time, it simply has to be able to dig tunnels.

HOW THE AFRICAN LUNGFISH BURROWS

The digging technique of this dipnoan is really unusual: it eats the slime as it digs its tunnel, taking it into its mouth and then expelling it through its gills. So, one bite after the other, the African lungfish digs its tunnel, which is usually vertical, widening toward the bottom. When it feels that water is becoming scarce, it rolls up on the bottom, and its skin secretes a substance that hardens, preventing its body from

drying when all the water has been vaporized. So, a sort of impermeable "cocoon" wraps around the animal and protects it, but a little hole is left open near the mouth to enable the creature to breathe just a little. The African lungfish can survive for up to four years inside its cocoon. So when it eventually finds itself in water again, it is usually quite lean; indeed, it becomes as thin as a rake if years go by. Therefore, its first problem is to put on some weight. But it is not a serious problem, for the animal eats anything, even plants, which it grinds with its strange plated teeth.

It is interesting to see that, at the beginning of August, even if an African lungfish is living in an aquarium, where water is always abundant, it becomes restless and starts digging. It is as if it had some sort of calendar inside it to warn it about the advent of the dry season.

HOW TO CATCH AN AFRICAN LUNGFISH

The meat of this fish is much appreciated, but catching an African lungfish is quite difficult. When the river is dry, the cocoons enclosing the fish cannot be seen. Moreover, when it swims, it is very shy and suspicious. But the people of Suda have discovered its weak point; they silently approach it habitat, and beat little drums with sticks, trying to imitate the noise of thunder. The fish reacts to these sounds by smacking its mouth, thus revealing itself to the cunning hunters.

11

6. THE PREADAPTATION OF RHIPIDISTIANS

In the previous chapters, we have tried to illustrate the features of the various sarcopterygians—fish that also use lungs to breathe—because they are the protagonists of the transition of vertebrates from aquatic to terrestrial life. It is from information on the anatomy of these animals, both living and fossil, that we can reconstruct this basic evolutionary transition, which is rather difficult to imagine, really. The idea that a teleost—a typical fish such as the perch—can leave the water and walk around in the fields seems quite absurd. This kind of fish has all the features needed for life in the water—and only in the water—which it cannot leave. But the sarcopterygians were totally different: they had been evolving for millions of years in warm, shallow waters lacking in oxygen, and which sometimes evaporated, leaving their inhabitants literally high and dry. This led to the creation of a kind of fish with anatomical structures extremely useful when it came to climbing out of the water and colonizing the dry land.

PREADAPTATION

Preadaptation is a very peculiar facet of evolution, and we are going to see it again in the transition from reptile to mammal.

Preadaptation means the growth of anatomical features useful both to the animal itself, and to the evolution in general. The evolution of sarcopterygians produced a fish which was not only adapted to its environment but also fit for leaving its environment, even though it was a little shy and awkward in the early days.

THE PREADAPTATION OF THE LIMB

The body of a fish is sustained by the water moved by the body itself; forward thrust is provided by the tail. The fins of a teleost are used only to correct rolling and pitching movements. They are wide and fanlike, and they have a light frame and bones that fan out. Sarcopterygians, on the other hand, also use their fins for locomotion on the slimy seabed. Indeed, as we have already seen, in dry periods, the rhipidistians could leave their puddles and crawl on their limbs to go off in search of deeper waters. So their fins were heavier, stumpier, and not fanlike; they had a stronger axis, and different bony parts on the sides.

The transformation of the fin into a limb has been closely studied using fossil finds. This research has revealed striking similarities between the frame of the fins of certain rhipidistians and the skeleton of the limbs of certain primitive amphibians, such as the *Ichthyostega*—the oldest amphibian we know. Actually, some parts of rhipidistians, owing to their position and features, can be considered the forerunners of the humerus, the femur, and the radius, and perhaps also the fingers. But the fact that the heavy, stumpy structure of the rhipidistian's fins help the creature to move on the ground is far more important than these similarities.

THE PREADAPTATION OF THE LUNG

We have already seen that sarcopterygians are able to breathe with their lungs as well. We have learnt this both from the study of living animals—the dipnoans—and from the fact that they breathe air through their nostrils, which open into the mouth by

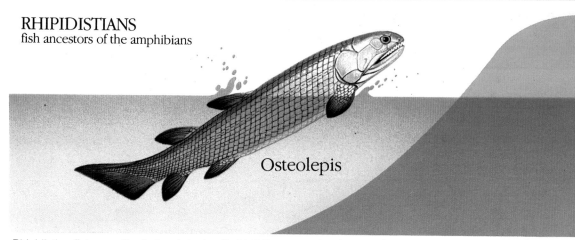

Rhipidistian fish were the first vertebrates that left the water, thanks to their functional and anatomical organization. The most typical fish, such as teleosts, absolutely cannot do this. Here, an *Osteolepis* is shown as a typical member of the group, though not as the protagonist of the transition.

means of the choanas. This new air duct required suitable bony structures, and we find them in fossils too. Rhipidistians already had their choanas, and lungs. Therefore, while still fish, they had this important anatomical structure absolutely necessary for living out of the water.

THE PREADAPTATION OF THE HEART

This is a more complex matter. The teleost's heart is not divided into a left and a right part, and only venous blood—which is pumped to the gills—passes through it. From the amphibians on, the heart is more or less completely separated into a right cavity—into which the venous blood for the gills flows—and a left cavity—perfused by arterial blood which has to reach

all the other parts of the body. This difference was apparently linked to the environments the two groups of animals lived in. Today, we do not know what kind of heart the rhipidistians had, for they are totally extinct. But among the living sarcopterygians, we can see that the hearts of both the *Latimeria* and the dipnoans are clearly divided into a right and a left part

and are crossed by two different kinds of blood. Hence, it is not rash to suppose that rhipidistians also had this important—but not essential—anatomical feature.

CONCLUSION

In Chapters 8 and 9 we are going to see which anatomical and functional features are needed for the transition from fish to amphibians. Some of them are particularly complex, others not so fundamental. The rhipidistians, owing to their acquisition of stumpy heavy fins, lungs for air breathing, and the double circulation of blood, are the best adapted—or rather preadapted—for the apparent, improbable transition from fish into amphibians.

TELEOSTS

Skeleton of a fin, and fin of a teleost, suitable only for movement in the water.

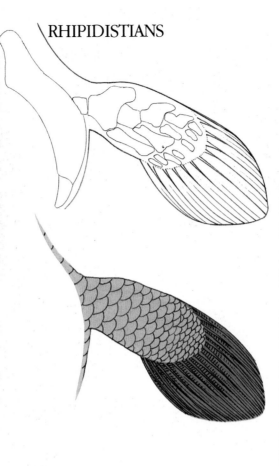

RHIPIDISTIANS

Skeleton of a fin, and pectoral fin of a rhipidistian (*Eusthenopteron*) with a rudimentary structure suitable for moving on slimy depths.

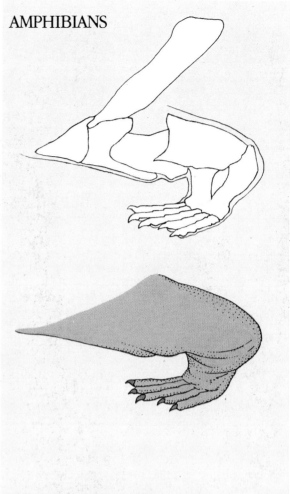

AMPHIBIANS

Skeleton of a leg, and foreleg of a primitive amphibian (*Ichthyostega*), suitable for moving on dry land.

RHIPIDISTIANS

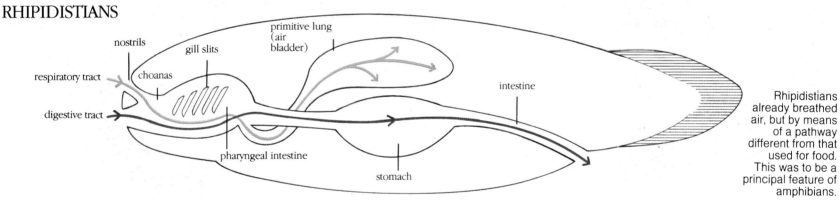

Rhipidistians already breathed air, but by means of a pathway different from that used for food. This was to be a principal feature of amphibians.

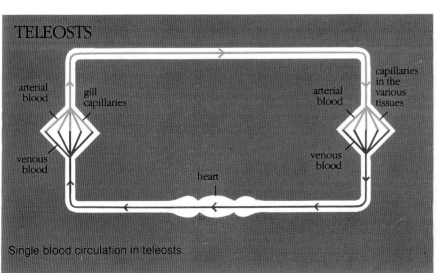

Single blood circulation in teleosts.

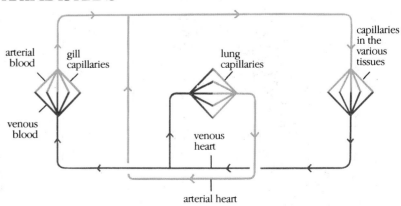

Double blood circulation in rhipidistians, which will be adopted by the amphibians.

Algae dominated the waters in the Silurian Period, around 420 million years ago. Some were huge, such as the sea tangles, here represented by two specimens of modern *Fucus*.

Lepidodendron

Sigillaria

7. THE STAGE THE AMPHIBIANS APPEARED ON

Amphibians—in Greek, the word means "double life," for they live both on the ground and in the water—appeared in the late Devonian Period, about 350 million years ago, but their debut was only possible because they had started living on the ground many millions of years earlier. In the middle of the Silurian Period, more than 420 million years ago, creatures were thriving in the water—more particularly, the vegetable kingdom, consisting of huge masses of large seaweeds, which we can still observe in the Sargasso Sea. The land above sea-level, on the other hand, must have been practically sterile, though not because of environmental conditions: oxygen was already abundant, and ozone was already protecting creatures against dangerous ultraviolet radiation; the only thing missing was food.

Animals were definitely not the ones to take that first step out of the water. Even though some of them tried it, or simply peeped out of the water, they soon slipped back into their environment—for that dry, rocky, lifeless landscape really was barren and unattractive.

ALGAE LEAVE THE WATER

Only plants could make the first move, for they can satisfy their need for food by themselves, thanks to

THE ADAPTATION OF PLANTS TO LIFE IN THE AIR

The vital problems of algae are easy to solve. All the plant's parts are self-dependent. They can absorb enough nourishment from the water and from the sun's rays to carry out photosynthesis and then release the oxygen they have produced. A plant living out of the water needs, in the first place, a skeletal structure capable of supporting the whole organism—in other words, a stem. Second, it needs something to take water and nourishment from the ground—that is to say, roots. Specialized parts, such as leaves and stems, are created for the purpose of effecting photosynthesis; but then, a system of vascular channels is needed to connect all the different parts. By means of vessels, roots are connected to leaves, which receive water and nourishment from the underground and can then synthetize the organic substance for distribution throughout the whole organism. Finally, the pores—or stomas—are the respiratory organs that plants use for taking carbon dioxide from the environment, processing it, and releasing oxygen. The first terrestrial plants, the psilophytales, did not have all these structures; they had no leaves. But most problems of terrestrial plants had now been solved.

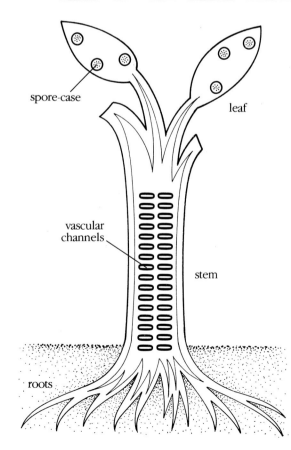

spore-case

leaf

vascular channels

stem

roots

Meganeura

Horsetails

Ferns

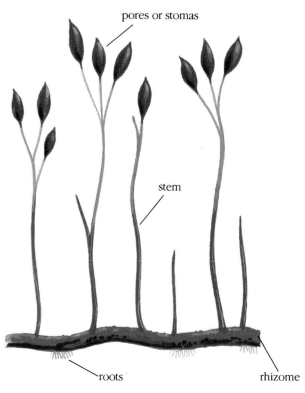

pores or stomas

stem

roots

rhizome

Psilophytales were the first plants that left the water, toward the end of the Silurian Period, 395 million years ago. This is the very ancient *Rhynia*, which already consisted of a stem, a spore case—that is, a capsule containing the spores for reproduction—and a creeping rhizome with small roots. Leaves did not exist yet.

In the Carboniferous Period, 340 million years ago, there were luxuriant forests, especially of club mosses (*Lepidodendron* and *Sigillaria*) up to 130 feet (40 meters) high and horsetails. Ferns made up the undergrowth. Gigantic invertebrates, such as the dragon *Meganeura*, already lived in this very humid habitat.

photosynthesis. Algae colonized the land above sea level, but why did they leave the water in the first place?

In the late Silurian Period, the Earth was shaken by strong orogenetic movements as the mountains were formed and emerged impressively from the sea and on the plains, and new lakes and swamps were formed. Consequently, certain algae had to face the problem of survival in an environment where there could sometimes be no water.

THE FIRST TERRESTRIAL PLANTS

But the transition from water to the land brought about extremely complex problems. Many attempts were probably made before the advent of a species capable of survival out of the water. Unfortunately, no fossil finds bear witness to such endeavors.

The oldest terrestrial plants we know are the psilophytales, such as the *Rhynia*. They already had stems—with vascular channels up to one and a half feet long (0.5 meters) running along the inside—and rhizomes—bunches of roots bearing buds—creeping along the ground. But there were no leaves, even though the stems of some of these plants did have slender, pricklelike protrusions, possibly the first attempt to produce leaves. They were definitely not

prickles, however, for there were no cropping animals around from which the plants had to defend themselves. The psilophytales were the first plants that managed to produce green areas on the ground, the first vegetable oases in what had once been a sterile, forbidding, and lifeless world.

FORESTS IN THE CARBONIFEROUS PERIOD

The spread of these first vascular plants did not last long. The appearance of more evolved species, with more highly differentiated and, therefore, more functional parts, led to the total extinction of the primitive family of psilophytales, the only evidence of which we have today are fossil remains. The newcomers long dominated the stage, and thronged the large forests in the Carboniferous Period; indeed, some of them have come down to us. The new plants were strong and massive. Club mosses and horsetails rose to 130 feet (40 meters); ferns were not taller than 50 feet (15 meters), for they preferred to enrich the undergrowth with shrubs, just as they do today. The exceptional thriving of flora in the Carboniferous Period seems to have been caused by the large amount of carbon dioxide in the atmosphere, produced by ongoing volcanic activity.

ANIMALS LEAVE THE WATER

In the thick of the scrub, in the tangled undergrowth, animals began to appear. The reason why they first left the waters must have been the great abundance of food on land: living or decaying vegetables. The invertebrates—very highly evolved—were the first to overcome the mythical border and started to spread unchallenged on dry land. Which were the first? We cannot answer this question, either. The first known terrestrial animals were scorpions, myriapods, and spiders, but very sophisticated species of insects—flying insects too—soon appeared in the Carboniferous Period. The abundance of food and the lack of predators led to the appearance of gigantic species, such as the *Meganeura*, a dragonfly with a wing spread of about 30 inches (75 centimeters)! This was the environment, or the stage, on which the amphibians at last made their debut.

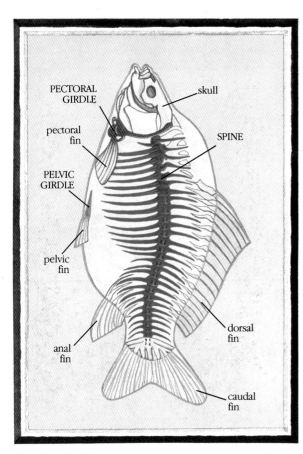

Skeleton of a fish.

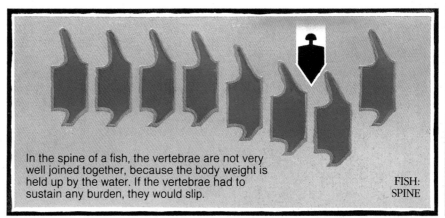

In the spine of a fish, the vertebrae are not very well joined together, because the body weight is held up by the water. If the vertebrae had to sustain any burden, they would slip.

FISH: SPINE

AMPHIBIAN: SPINE

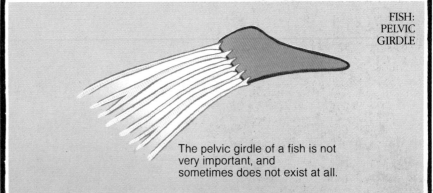

FISH: PELVIC GIRDLE

AMPHIBIAN: PELVIC GIRDLE

The pelvic girdle of a fish is not very important, and sometimes does not exist at all.

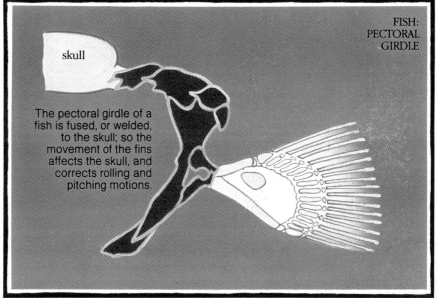

skull

The pectoral girdle of a fish is fused, or welded, to the skull; so the movement of the fins affects the skull, and corrects rolling and pitching motions.

FISH: PECTORAL GIRDLE

AMPHIBIAN: PECTORAL GIRDLE

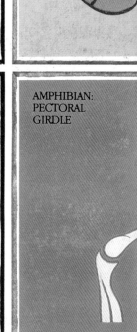

The schematized colors of the various parts of a fish and of an amphibian (above) are repeated in the overall views on the left and on the right.

8. WHAT MAKES AN AMPHIBIAN: THE SKELETON

At the beginning of the Carboniferous Period, about 350 million years ago, the water and the land were very rich in life, mostly in the areas with tropical climates, as we saw in the previous chapter. More particularly, the rhipidistians were already able to take short walks out of the water. Almost certainly, during that period, the great abundance of food in the undergrowth—which was abundantly available, since there were no direct competitors—strongly urged these creatures to stay out of the water, at least during the hunting season. Probably, this was the real reason for the appearence of amphibians, but the path that led toward the transition from fish to amphibian is still very long.

PREADAPTATION

The phenomenon of preadaptation (see Chapter 6), is very important for an understanding of this transformation. Due to environmental selection, rhipidistians had acquired extremely precious anatomical features that enabled them to live out of the water. Such features, however, were not enough to create an amphibian; other changes had to take place.

CHANGES IN THE SPINE

When the fish's body is sustained by the water, the spine is only used for movement; it bends, to flick the tail, for instance. But when that same body leaves the water, all its weight is discharged onto the spine, which must be stiff and mobile at the same time. In fish, vertebrae are not very well joined together. In amphibians they are embedded one into the other, so that they do not slip when they have to support a weight or push. This important modification must take place in any animal that leaves the water, even if it only has to crawl for a short time. Rhipidistians had already solved the problem by inclining their vertebral arches, so that each vertebra lay on another. But starting from the amphibians, vertebrae acquired inferior and superior articular processes in the vertebral arch (zygapophyses), which gave the spinal column a rigid continuity. In the most developed amphibians and in reptiles the vertebrae articulate as well. Thus the spine becomes even stronger and is able to sustain exceptional weights, as in certain huge herbivorous dinosaurs.

The interdependence between these articulations and terrestrial life is further proved by the fact that, if the animal goes back to live in the water—as dolphins did—then it loses its articulations, and its vertebrae are no longer embedded in one another.

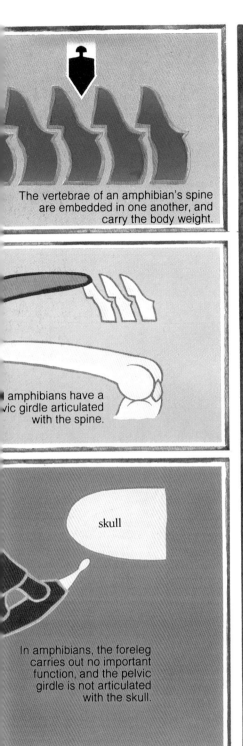

The vertebrae of an amphibian's spine are embedded in one another, and carry the body weight.

amphibians have a
vic girdle articulated
with the spine.

In amphibians, the foreleg carries out no important function, and the pelvic girdle is not articulated with the skull.

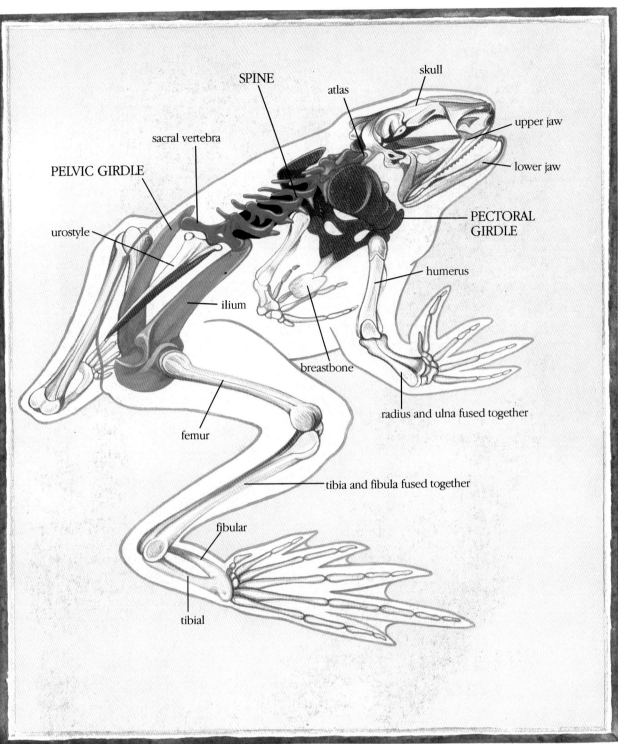

Skeleton of an amphibian (frog).

THE GIRDLES CHANGE

Fish are moved only by the thrust their tails produce; the pectoral fins are there to correct the body's position, which is otherwise changed by rolling and pitching motions; therefore, the pectoral girdle is attached to the skull by means of bony parts. The pelvic girdle, where the other two fins articulate, is not very important, and some fish do not even have it.

For an animal living out of the water, the tail is relatively unimportant for movement, and the creature does not have to cope with problems of rolling and pitching; forward thrust is essentially provided by the movement of the hind legs. This causes a real revolution in the joints between skeleton, girdles, and limbs. The pectoral girdle loses

its importance and does not articulate with the skull any more—only the most primitive amphibians still have this articulation—while the pelvic girdle—in order to discharge the movement of the hind legs onto the spine, and so onto the whole body—is connected with one or more vertebrae, now called sacral vetebrae, by means of a bony part called the ilium.

Unless an animal crawls or slithers—a snake, for example—or swims—a cetacean, let us say—all terrestrial vetebrates must have these skeletal articulations.

On the other hand, there is no trace of such articulations in the rhipidistians, and they must therefore be regarded as new acquisitions, typical of the amphibians and of all the animals derived from them.

THE INVENTION OF THE NECK

Fish have no neck: a fish is unable to move its head to the right and to the left because its skull is fused with its spinal column. To turn its head, it must move all its trunk, more or less as we do when we have a stiff neck. Conversely, amphibians were the first to have their skulls articulated with the first vertebra, the atlas, so that the head could move from side to side; from here on, it is possible to speak of a true and proper neck. One curiosity: in this case, too, when a reptile or mammal—such as the ichthyosaur, or the whale—goes back to life in the water, the skull becomes stiff on the spine again, and we cannot speak of a neck any longer.

The reason for this has still to be discovered.

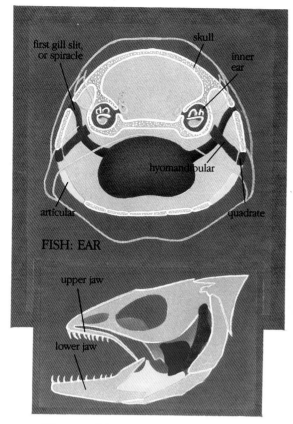

FISH: EAR

Diagram of the skulls of a fish (above) and of an amphibian (right). The picture on top shows them frontally, in cross-section; the picture below shows them from the side. The color helps to highlight the bony parts of the ear. Fish have ears, but not hearing, whereas amphibians are able to perceive sounds. In order to do that, they have adapted bony parts that are also present in the skull of the fish.

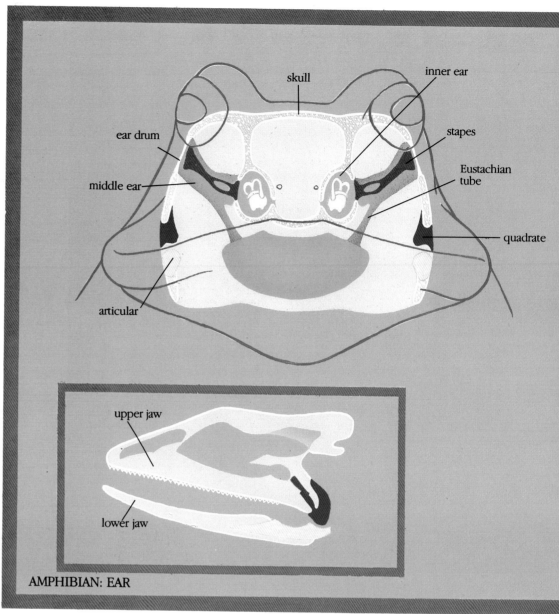

AMPHIBIAN: EAR

9. WHAT MAKES AN AMPHIBIAN: THE EAR AND THE EYE

THE EAR OF A FISH

Fish have perfect, very sensitive hearing, but it is provided by their lateral line, and not by their ears, as we saw in the *Marine Life* volume of this series. Their ears are mere semicircular canals—the utricle and the saccule—and their only function is to solve problems of balance; they cannot perceive sounds. This last function is carried out by the living cells of the lateral line, which interpret sound vibrations in water. In an adult amphibian that lives out of water, these cells are no longer sensitive; the skin hardens and becomes rich in keratin to avoid desiccation, and it becomes impossible to have perfectly living cells exposed to the environment. A new organ is needed, but what should it be like?

THE LOWER JAW

Strange as it may seem, it is the lower jaw or, rather, the joint mechanism which links the lower jaw with the skull, that is involved in the formation of ears that

hear. The same thing will later happen to mammals. In fish, the lower jaw is articulated with the skull by means of a bone, the hyomandibular. Most fish have this kind of jaw-joint, which suddenly changes, however, in the transition to the amphibian.

THE EAR OF THE AMPHIBIAN

The amphibian's ear has a small bone, the stapes, the outer edge of which rests on a thin, transparent membrane, the ear drum (or tympanum), and its inner side is near the outer ear. Here, near the old semicircular canals—utricle and saccule—there is a new, sensitive part: the lagena. To be brief, the sound wave makes the eardrum vibrate, and the vibration is then transmitted by the stapes to the inner ear, where it is perceived by the lagena. These parts are not new: fish had them, but they were used for a different purpose. The stapes is the result of a transformation of the hyomandibular bone, a part of the fish jaw-joint. And the cavity in which the stapes lies—the inner ear and the Eustachian tube—derives from the gill

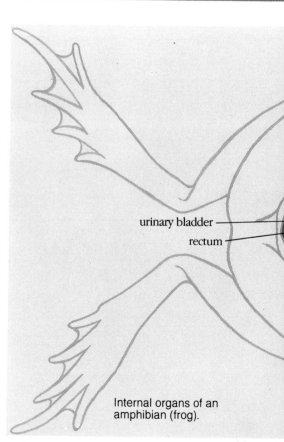

Internal organs of an amphibian (frog).

18

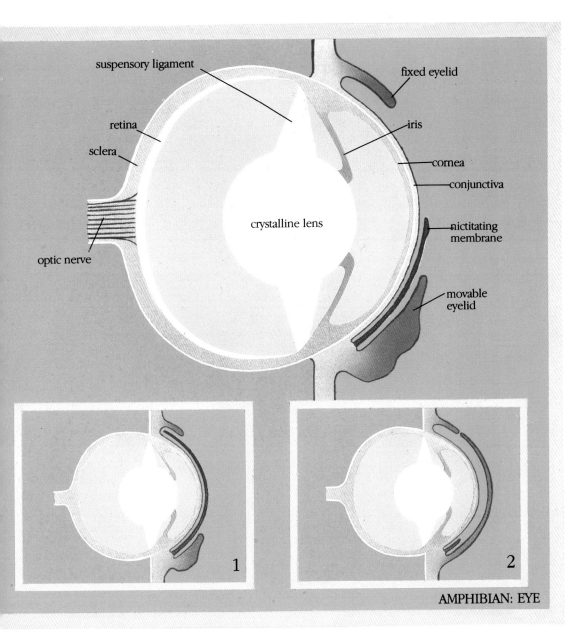

suspensory ligament

fixed eyelid

retina

iris

sclera

cornea

conjunctiva

crystalline lens

nictitating membrane

optic nerve

movable eyelid

1

2

AMPHIBIAN: EYE

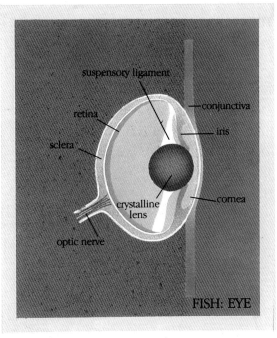

suspensory ligament

conjunctiva

retina

iris

sclera

crystalline lens

cornea

optic nerve

FISH: EYE

Diagram of a side cross-section of the eyes of a fish (above) and of an amphibian (left). These organs are functional in both animals, and change only slightly in the transition from water to land: tear glands and eyelids form.

The two insets on the left show the movements of the nictitant membrane (1) and of the lower eyelid (2) of an amphibian's eye. Both are movable, and cover und uncover the eyeball, to keep it wet and clean, and to protect it.

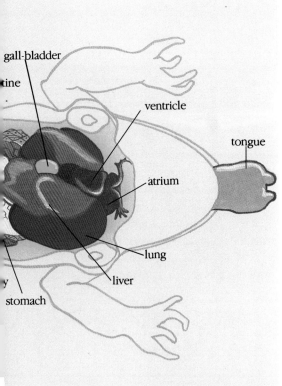

gall-bladder

tine

ventricle

tongue

atrium

lung

liver

y

stomach

chamber. Only the sensitive part—the lagena—is a new organ, though it is still connected with the old part of the ear: the vestibular apparatus. While studying a frog or a toad, it is easy to see the eardrum behind the eye; it is made up of a round, and often differently colored, area of skin. This is the beginning of the amphibian's hearing ear.

THE EYE

In the transition from water to land, the eye in itself does not change, but acquires new structures to allow it to work out of the water as well. In fish, the front part of the eye—the conjunctiva and the cornea—is made up of living cells that connect with the cells of the skin around the eye. But out of the water, the problem is that the eye might dry up. Usually, the skin cells prevent this danger by hardening and producing abundant keratin. But this is not possible for the cells of the outer eye, which always must be alive and transparent—their hornification would make them opaque, and the animal would become blind. The problem is solved by a veil of liquid covering the animal's eye, just as if it were in the water.

EYELIDS AND TEAR GLANDS

To cover the front part of the eye, the animal uses some folded skin; indeed, amphibians have three skin folds on their eyes: the nictitating membrane—which we humans do not have—is thin, nearly transparent, and adheres to the eye; the others, the upper and lower lids, are thicker and have the same color as the animal. Both the nictitating membrane and the lower lid run across the eyeball, covering and uncovering it. Moreover, certain glands secrete a watery substance, which is continuously spread over the eye, so that its cells can stay alive and do their job perfectly in the aerial environment too.

TEARS

Tears or, rather, the lachrymal liquid, appear for the first time in amphibians, and accomplish the specific task of producing an aquatic environment around the eye. But tears carry out another equally important function: if they did not contain an excellent antibacterial and fungicidal agent—the so-called lysozym—the eye cells would be a very fertile reproduction ground for bacteria, viruses, and funguses. Thanks to this substance, the eye is also protected against the attack of microorganisms, which continuously infiltrate under an animal's eyelids.

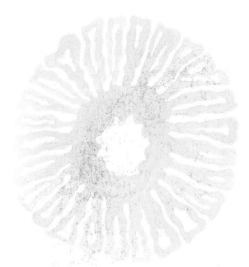

One of the many features shared by rhipidistian fish, the amphibians' ancestors (such as *Eusthenopteron*), and the most ancient amphibians (such as *Ichthyostega*) is the labyrinth-like structure of their tooth enamel, which is shown in section above.

The most ancient imprint of a primitive amphibian, recently found in Brazil.

The *Ichthyostega* is the most ancient amphibian known to date: it lived during the Devonian Period and its body, especially its head, still had fishlike features. The reason for this is that the animal lived a life very close to water.

10. THE FIRST AMPHIBIANS APPEAR: THE ICHTHYOSTEGA

THE LABYRINTH TOOTH

Evidence of the similarity between rhipidistian fish and the most primitive amphibians is provided by the skeletal structure of skull and fin, and also by the structure of the tooth. Among all vertebrates, these two groups are the only ones which have a peculiar, ivory-covered tooth: the outer part—the ivory—penetrates inside, into the dentine, forming a strange pattern which, in cross-section, looks much like a labyrinth. This is why the first amphibians are named labyrinthodonts (having labyrinth-like teeth).

THE FIRST AMPHIBIAN

Until recently, it was believed that the date and place of birth of the first amphibian were, respectively, the beginning of the Carboniferous Period, 340 million years ago, and Gondwanaland, the primitive supercontinent that was later to divide and form Africa, Australia, Antarctica, South America, India and Madagascar. Recently, however, the imprint of an amphibian has been found in Brazil, in ground that dates back to 360 million years ago. With this discovery, it may be possible to state that the amphibians first appeared in South America toward the end of the Devonian Period, and that they later spread all over the Earth.

The amphibian that left its imprint in the Devonian mud in Brazil has been named *Notopus petri*, but we know absolutely nothing about it. The oldest amphibian of which we have found the fossil skeleton is the *Ichthyostega*. This first known specimen of four-legged animals was found in Greenland, where the climate, at the end of the Devonian Period, was obviously totally different from today, since it was inhabited by amphibians that liked a constant, wet climate. *Ichthyostega*, over 3 feet (1 meter) long—quite a large animal, then—is too large to be regarded as a forerunner of the amphibians. We have already pointed out, and we will see later on, that the phenomenon of giantism occurs within an expanding group with no direct rivals to compete with. So *Ichthyostega* is already an advanced amphibian in the evolutionary process, and not the connecting link with fish. It still has some fishlike features, such as the massive, powerful skull and the large mouth typical of a predator. Its favorite food was probably fish, since its weak limbs and strong tail made it easier to move quickly in the water than on land. Out of the liquid element, it could hunt only rather slow prey, such as gastropods (snails), annelids (worms), and larvae. Its general features, as a matter of fact, reveal that this animal did not really walk, but crawled on the ground with a snakelike movement. Much time went by before it learned how to walk well and fast on the ground.

The evolution of the amphibian class, begun with these animals, did not take place gradually; it was rapid, explosive even, and alternated with slower stages. But not all the features of the true amphibians developed progressively; many of them appeared out of the blue, when the animals still had fishlike features. This kind of evolution is called *patchwork*, a suitable term, and we will see a typical example of it in Chapter 28.

Skeleton of *Ichthyostega*.

Ichthyostega

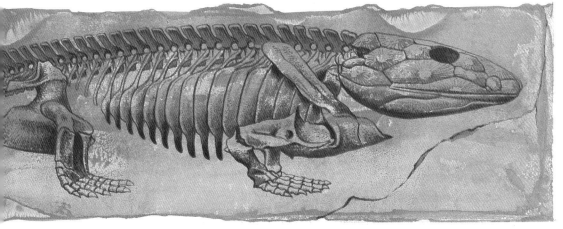

There is a science, called "ichnology", which studies the imprints left on the ground in the different geological eras. From these imprints, it is possible to glean interesting information about the features of the animals that left them, and their ways of moving. The first amphibians probably walked very clumsily; their trunks were still very stumpy and heavy, whereas their limbs were small and weak, certainly unable to sustain their body weight. Thus, these animals had to crawl with a snakelike movement, more or less as today's newts and salamanders do. Even the oldest known amphibians had hind legs that were stronger and more powerful than the forelegs, totally unlike the fins of the fish, as we have already seen. Their legs moved one at a time; one moved forward, while the other three stayed still on the ground. For instance, they moved the right front leg first, and then the left hind leg; then the left front leg, and finally, the right hind leg.

This way of moving caused a marked twisting of the spinal column, and the head swung from side to side. To change and improve this ungainly gait, it would be necessary to modify the articulations of legs and pelvis, but this was only to occur in the most advanced reptiles.

11. THE ERA OF THE AMPHIBIANS

(Labyrinthodonts)

In the late Devonian Period, 350 million years ago, the Earth was already inhabited by the first true amphibians—including *Ichthyostega*, as a typical representative—that belonged to a large group, or subclass, of fossil amphibians, which were called labyrinthodonts.

THE LABYRINTHODONTS

These amphibians owe their name to their teeth, as we have seen in Chapter 10. Quite rapidly, they spread over all the Earth, aided by the fact that land above sea level in the Devonian Period formed one single supercontinent. So even though they were very bad walkers, the labyrinthodonts managed to settle over all the Earth, especially in the areas with a torrid climate and abundant water. In point of fact, labyrinthodonts probably did not like the terrestrial life very much, since even the most advanced specimens had stumpy, heavy bodies and huge skulls; besides, their legs were still too weak, having insufficient muscles, whereas their tails were usually sturdy and strong. All these features lead us to believe that labyrinthodonts preferred an aquatic environment to dry land.

THEIR DEVELOPMENT

Labyrinthodonts may have been the primitive amphibians which, better than any other group, managed to survive the harshness of their environment and the appearance of other, more advanced animals. They first appeared in the late Devonian Period, and developed especially in the Carboniferous Period, when most of the Earth was covered by immense tropical forests. But they managed to survive even when climatic conditions became very hard, during the Permian Period, and they were still present almost at the end of the Jurassic Period, around 140 million years ago. These amphibians lived together with the dinosaurs of the Cenozoic, or Tertiary Era and they dwelled on the Earth's surface for over 200 million years!

GILLED AMPHIBIANS

A few small-sized labyrinthodonts, such as *Gerrothorax* and *Branchiosaurus*, have three pairs of long, feathery gills at the sides of their heads. The paleontologists who have studied these animals cannot reach an agreement. Some regard them as labyrinthodonts that went back to live in the water for good, and the gills seem to be sure evidence of this; others think that the animals in question were merely larval forms, destined to lose their gills with metamorphosis, and then become more terrestrial amphibians. The discussion is still open, and it does not seem that a solution is near, even though the latter theory seems less likely; for these animals already had well-formed legs that worked perfectly, and that is something larvae never have.

Archeria

Micropholis

Left: skull of *Neopteroplax*, a labyrinthodont of the Carboniferous Period.

THE POLYPHYLETIC ORIGIN OF THE AMPHIBIANS

All experts agree that *Ichthyostega* is the oldest amphibian we know to date; but not all consider it as the founder of the whole class. It is doubtful whether amphibians originated from a single group of rhipidistian fish. Extinct and living amphibians are so different from each other that the hypothesis of subsequent passages from water to land of different forms of rhipidistian fish is justifiable. From these, later, the different evolutionary lines of amphibians developed independently. So this class many be polyphyletic; that is, it may derive from more than one ancestral line. This is not surprising, if we take into account how easy it is for a fish that is also capable of breathing air to become an amphibian.

Capitosaurus

Cacops

Eryops

THE TAIL GETS SHORTER

As the years went by, labyrinthodonts acquired new features which made them fitter for living out of the water. The tail, which was very useful for swimming, but quite inconvenient for walking on land, gradually became shorter. In *Cacops*, it was already shorter, compared with older specimens; in *Eryops*, it was practically just a stump.

These specimens were probably improving their adaptation to terrestrial life step by step, but their stout bodies and small limbs show that they moved slowly or crawled.

THE GIANT LABYRINTHODONT

By going back to live in the water, some amphibians were able to increase the size and weight of their bodies considerably, in spite of the slender skeletal structure of their limbs. *Trematosaurus* and *Mastodonsaurus*, which lived in the Triassic Period, reached lengths of 10 to 16 feet (3 to 5 meters), and they must have been fierce predators, judging by their hefty skulls. This is more or less what happened with the giant herbivorous dinosaurs: they, too, went back to live in the water, which could support the enormous weight of their bodies more efficiently. Only in this way were both the amphibians and the dinosaurs able to overcome the shortcomings of their skeletons and limbs.

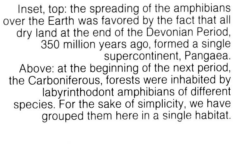

Inset, top: the spreading of the amphibians over the Earth was favored by the fact that all dry land at the end of the Devonian Period, 350 million years ago, formed a single supercontinent, Pangaea.
Above: at the beginning of the next period, the Carboniferous, forests were inhabited by labyrinthodont amphibians of different species. For the sake of simplicity, we have grouped them here in a single habitat.

Right: some amphibians went back into the water for good, as we see from their gills, which detached just behind the skull.

Mastodonsaurus

Left: *Mastodonsaurus* was one of the labyrinthodonts that went back to live in water. It lived in the Triassic Period, about 220 million years ago, and had an impressive size for an amphibian: it reached a length of 10 feet (3 meters), with an enormous skull 5 feet (1.5 meters) long. Its huge bulk was held up by the water, in which the animal spent most of its time, hunting its favorite food, fish. Fossils of *Mastodonsaurus* have been found in Germany and Africa.

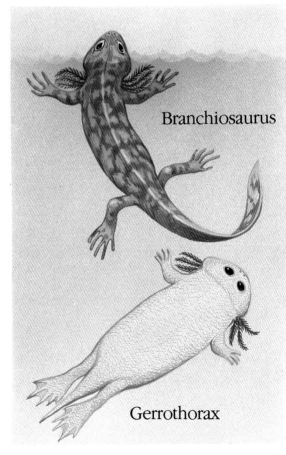

Branchiosaurus

Gerrothorax

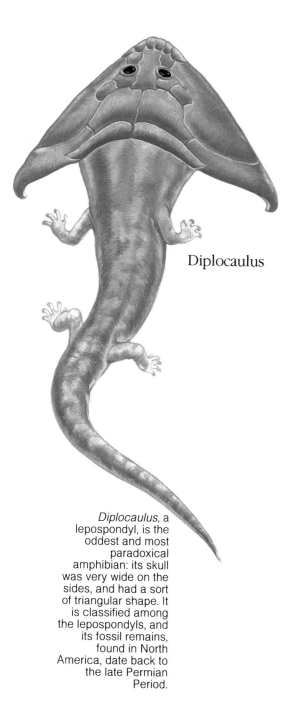

Diplocaulus

Diplocaulus, a lepospondyl, is the oddest and most paradoxical amphibian: its skull was very wide on the sides, and had a sort of triangular shape. It is classified among the lepospondyls, and its fossil remains, found in North America, date back to the late Permian Period.

12. LONGER BODIES
(Lepospondyls)

Microbrachis

A group of amphibians of the Carboniferous Period, the lepospondyls, present a phenomenon we will find again only very late in the reptile class: the body becomes longer, the number of vertebrae in the spine increases, whereas the limbs become smaller, and finally disappear.

LIMBS ARE LOST

The body thus becomes snakelike, and crawls on the ground with an undulatory movement. This is quite a surprising phenomenon, since the stumpy and heavy bodies of the amphibians in the Carboniferous Period, with their small legs, certainly allowed very little freedom of movement. These animals had to

crawl on the ground by twisting their backbones (as we saw in Chapter 10), and this was already a basis for future snakelike movements. The lepospondyls do not only include species with exceptionally long bodies and very small, insignificant legs, such as *Microbrachis* and *Hyloplesion*; there are also species with snakelike features, such as *Phlegethontia*.

BUT ALL IS NOT YET CLEAR

So apparently, everything seems easy, straightforward and logical: lepospondyls progressively acquired snakelike features, increasing the number of their vertebrae, so that their bodies became longer; then, their limbs became smaller and smaller, until they

disappeared altogether in the most advanced and developed specimens.

Unfortunately, the lepospondyl specimens we know of do not confirm this sequence; more particularly, *Phlegethontia*, the limbless species with a snakelike body, is no younger than the other forms; on the contrary, it came before them. So the limbless specimen is older than the one that still has small legs.

ANOTHER MYSTERY

Phlegethontia deserve further discussion, for the skeletons of these little, inconspicuous animals date back as early as the beginning of the Carboniferous Period, when the amphibian adventure started. This

Phlegethontia

Hyloplesion

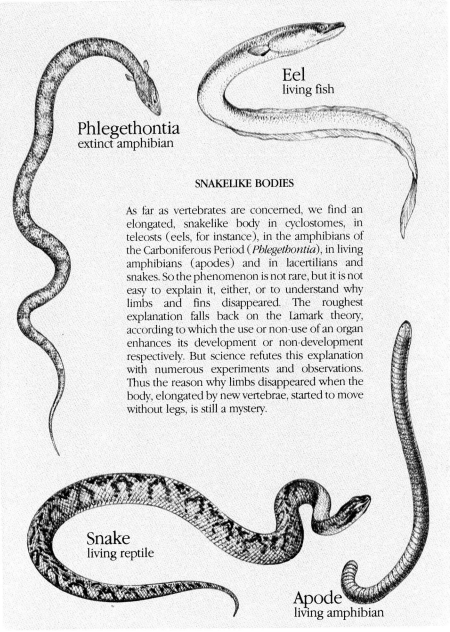

Phlegethontia
extinct amphibian

Eel
living fish

SNAKELIKE BODIES

As far as vertebrates are concerned, we find an elongated, snakelike body in cyclostomes, in teleosts (eels, for instance), in the amphibians of the Carboniferous Period (*Phlegethontia*), in living amphibians (apodes) and in lacertilians and snakes. So the phenomenon is not rare, but it is not easy to explain it, either, or to understand why limbs and fins disappeared. The roughest explanation falls back on the Lamark theory, according to which the use or non-use of an organ enhances its development or non-development respectively. But science refutes this explanation with numerous experiments and observations. Thus the reason why limbs disappeared when the body, elongated by new vertebrae, started to move without legs, is still a mystery.

Snake
living reptile

Apode
living amphibian

Some species of more modest size developed among the amphibians of the Carboniferous Period. These smaller animals had very long tails and bodies, and are classified as lepospondyls by scholars. There were not many of them, and some looked like salamanders and had four short legs. Others, similar to snakes, had no limbs at all, and moved by undulating their spinal column. The *Phlegethontia*, which returned to live in water for good, was one of these.

apodal—or limbless—creature must have had forerunners with fins or limbs, and evolution must have taken millions of years to eliminate them. But if we say this, then we have to push the appearance of the amphibians many millions of years back in time. This proves how many things remain to be studied and discovered in the field of paleontology.

THE SURVIVORS

Lepospondyls inhabited the swampy forests of North America and Europe during the Carboniferous Period. However, they probably preferred aquatic environments or, at any rate, life very close to the water, with soft ground they could burrow into also, to

find nourishment. All lepospondyls disappeared between the Carboniferous and the Permian Period, when the climate changed dramatically. There might have been animals deriving from them, but we do not know of any fossil remains that might link these ancient amphibians to the presentday apodes, which are limbless and love torrid, temperate climates, too (see Chapter 20).

A STRANGE AMPHIBIAN

But the story of the lepospondyls does not end here: other species of them appeared, and they were similar to the salamanders we know today, although they did have strange, enormous, paradoxical skulls. One of

them was the *Diplocaulus*. The side parts of the skull are swollen, giving it a triangular shape with two round eyes projecting from it. It is not easy to answer the question of why that skull was so strange, why it had such an unusual shape, for no animal belonging to any class has ever had a skull like it. The only possible hypothesis seems to be that the skull was used to dig into the mud, or soft ground, to unearth animals; but it is still a mystery, really.

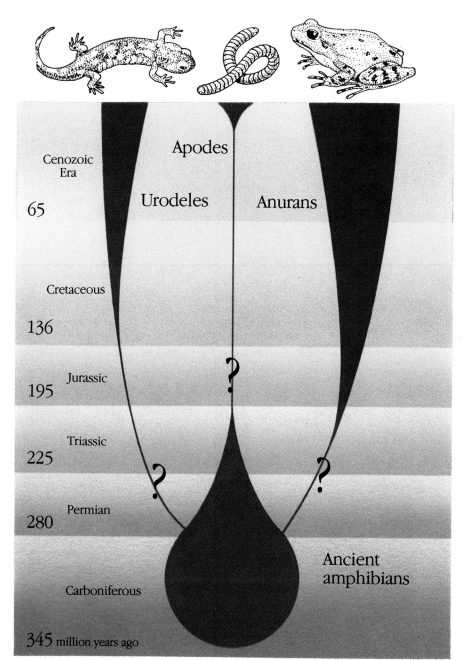

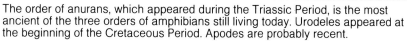

The order of anurans, which appeared during the Triassic Period, is the most ancient of the three orders of amphibians still living today. Urodeles appeared at the beginning of the Cretaceous Period. Apodes are probably recent.

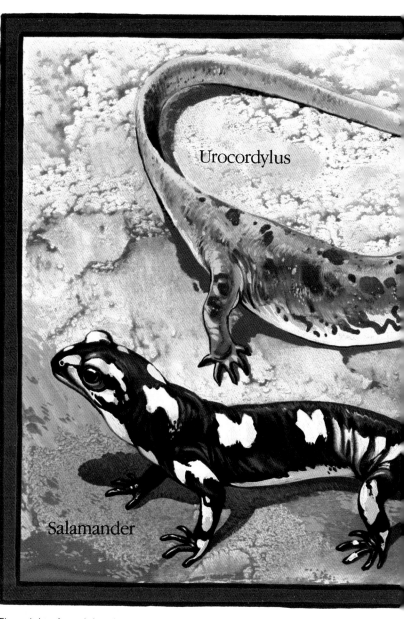

The origin of urodeles, here represented by a salamander, is not yet certain. One of the probable suspects could be *Urocordylus*, now extinct.

13. THE ORIGINS OF LIVING AMPHIBIANS

Today, there are three orders of amphibians in the world: *Urodela* (with tails)—such as the salamander and the newt—*Anura* (without tails)—the frog and the toad—and *Apoda* (without limbs)—almost unknown amphibians with bodies similar to those of earthworms. We shall call them urodeles, anurans, and apodes. The features of these animals are very peculiar, and cannot be compared. For instance, urodeles show a marked regression; that is to say that their organs are reduced or simplified; while anurans are exceptionally well-evolved amphibians. If we examine a frog, we can see that its hind legs are the best adapted to jumping of all the vertebrates. On the other hand, apodes are really mysterious with their strange, invertebrate bodies.

THE ORIGINS

The problem of linking presentday amphibians to those which ruled during the Carboniferous Period has not been satisfactorily solved yet. We can only make hypotheses. On thing is sure, however: in that Period, the Earth was inhabited by hundreds of different species of amphibians, small and huge, but there were no frogs or toads, or newts or salamanders. But the riddle of the relationship between the living and the old amphibians is being tackled by studying the structure of the vertebrae.

THE ORIGINS OF URODELES

This order of amphibians definitely appeared in the early Cretaceous Period. There is a 60-million-year gap between the end of old amphibians and the beginning of urodeles; no urodele fossils have been found to bridge the gap, making it extremely difficult to establish the origins of this order. Lepospondyls show the most resemblances. A good example is

Urocordylus, which lived in the Carboniferous Peric Examining the skeletal features and the reconstructe shape of this old amphibian, we cannot help noting it similarity with presentday urodeles. Indeed, th animal seems to have been nimbler and livelier, as th long tail with its flattened sides—very useful fc swimming—tends to prove. But we already know tha urodeles are regressed animals, with less ossifie skeletons; few, weak muscles; and they are slow an awkward movers.

The evolution which has led to the present new and salamanders is thought to have started from th *Urocordylus*, or from its close relatives.

THE ORIGINS OF ANURANS

These amphibians seem to be older than urodele Maybe their evolutionary line started when all the ol amphibians disappeared. Study of the anuran

We can establish at least three basic stages in the evolution of the anurans. The most ancient specimen, *Miobatrachus*, lived perhaps in the Carboniferous Period; *Triadobatrachus*, definitely an anuran, lived in the Triassic Period; *Neobatrachus*, of the Jurassic Period, was already a frog, and could jump.

...orefathers is made easier by certain peculiarities of their skeletons, such as the spine, which is short, has few vertebrae and no tail—whence the name anuran; the elongated bones of the pelvis; and the peculiar hind limbs and flattened skull.

THE METHODS
OF PALEONTOLOGICAL RESEARCH

The search for the ancestors of the frog gives us an opportunity to understand how we must go back in time to try and find some link between different animals living in different times. The skeleton of a frog is so personal and characteristic that even the layman can easily recognize it.

Starting from today's frog, we go back and seek animals that had similar skeletons. Up to 150 million years ago, we can consider the problem solved, for the skeleton of *Neobatrachus* has all the features of a frog or a toad: its skull is flattened and has wide openings; its spine does not end in a tail, but in a bony stick—called urostyle; the pelvic bones are very large; and in its long hind legs, tibia and fibula are fused together. There can be no doubt about it: the *Neobatrachus* is an anuran. It is therefore logical to imagine a landscape in the Jurassic Period, with terrible, huge dinosaurs, but also harmless frogs leaping to and fro around them.

Let's go further back in time. In the Triassic Period, 200 million years ago, we meet the *Triadobatrachus*, with a froglike skull, pelvis, and short tail, and with conventional, not specialized, legs. This is still an anuran, not yet specialized for jumping, but it soon will be.

So far, so good, but if we go back a little further, doubts begin to arise, and we are not so certain about our conclusions. Looking at amphibian skeletons of the Carboniferous Period, we do not see any typical frog feature. We gather vague hints in the *Miobatrachus*, which lived 300 million years ago. Its pelvis is a little strange and its tail is small, while its skull is massive and heavy. This creature could be the link between the first amphibians and the evolutionary line of anurans, but we cannot be sure about it. What we can safely say, however, is that the evolution of anurans, which has led to our present frogs and toads, started in the Triassic Period with the *Triadobatrachus*.

14. THE FEATURES OF AMPHIBIANS: METAMORPHOSIS

When a living creature, or larva, emerges from an egg, and at some stage of its life completely changes its anatomical features and its life-style, we are dealing with the process called metamorphosis. This phenomenon was first evident in invertebrates. We all know how a greyish, creeping caterpillar turns into a brightly colored, gracefully flying butterfly.

In vertebrates the phenomenon is less common. Indeed, according to the rules of the game, when an animal is hatched, small as it may be, it should already have all the features of the adult. But every rule has its exception: hence, there are different kinds of metamorphoses in cyclostomes, dipnoans and amphibians. The metamorphosis of cyclostomes and dipnoans—fish—is not so revolutionary, for only a few structures change in the transition from larva to fish.

The metamorphosis of amphibians, on the other hand, is far more interesting.

EXTRAORDINARY SIMILARITY

As we have seen in the previous chapters, the origin of amphibians is to be found among rhipidistian fish, which are extinct today. And among the amphibians closest living relatives we have the dipnoans, the only fish to undergo metamorphosis! Indeed, dipnoans are so similar to amphibians, it is almost as if they wanted to show they are related.

THE EGGS OF AMPHIBIANS

Usually, the animals belonging to this class simply lay their eggs in the outside environment, and then leave them to their fate—but we shall see that there are exceptions here as well. These creatures, especially the anurans, generally have their eggs packed together in a mass of jelly, which protects them against both the hazards of the environment and against hungry predators, for most animals seem to dislike this mucilaginous substance. Toads are perhaps the the tidiest: they produce two long strings of jelly containing eggs, lined up in rows, like a pearl necklace.

THE DEVELOPMENT OF THE AMPHIBIAN

After a generally short period of time, then, the larva hatches—rather rapidly, too. At birth the amphibian is very similar to a fish in its anatomical structure and in its functions. Its skin, gills, heart, blood circulation,

and metabolism are typical of a fish. If it is provided with lungs, they are very small, and are not used. The larval stage can last from few months to more than one year. If environmental conditions—temperature and nourishment—are not suitable, development stops. If all goes well, metamorphosis begins.

METAMORPHOSIS

Metamorphosis fascinates us all, especially researchers. In just a few months, an organism with all the features of a fish turns into a little animal that can live out of water. The limbs grow; the lungs start to work; in anurans the long tail disappears. All the organs undergo transformation, so that at the end of the process, a completely new organism—quite different from the previous one—has developed.

Metamorphosis sums up the history of amphibians. If we observe what takes place during the metamorphosis of an anuran—frog or toad—we will be impressed by the similarity of this process with the transition from fish to amphibian, which took place more than 300 million years ago, when the structure of the fish made it into an organism that could live out of water.

THE LARVA OF THE AMPHIBIAN

When the larva hatches, it is like a fish, but it has fewer needs. Its mouth has horny little teeth, so that the creature can also feed on the weeds that cover stones in rivers or ponds. These larvae can really eat anything, flesh even, and if nothing else is available, they can eat what adult amphibians and fish would never dream of touching. Larvae feed on things that tempt no other animal, so they have no competition to contend with. They do have many enemies, but the large number of eggs and larvae compensates for this.

EXCEPTIONS

Metamorphosis is a typical feature of amphibians, but the stages are not all alike. We will see that some amphibian parents look after their offspring or have close relationships with them. Moreover, the embryo of the *Breviceps adspersus*, a frog that lives in the dry areas of South Africa, completes its development and goes through metamorphosis while still inside its protective mass of jelly. So when it decides to venture outside, it is already grown up.

40 million years

Latimeria
coelacanth

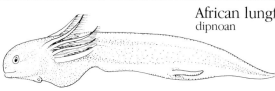

African lung[
dipnoan

South Americ[
lungfish
dipnoan

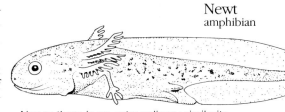

Newt
amphibian

Above: there is an extraordinary similarity between the larvae of the dipnoan fish and those of the amphibians. This gives evidence of their distant kinship.

about 4 months

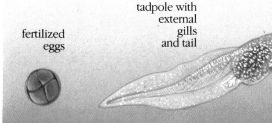

fertilized
eggs

tadpole with
external
gills
and tail

The metamorphosis of an anuran amphibian (below, the development of an edible frog) seems to sum up in a few months what occurred over 3000 million years ago (top), when the amphibians evolved from crossopterygian fish, more particularly, from the rhipidistians. This slow process probably lasted about 40 million years.

Holoptychius
rhipidistian

Ichthyostega
amphibian

Mastodonsaurus
amphibian

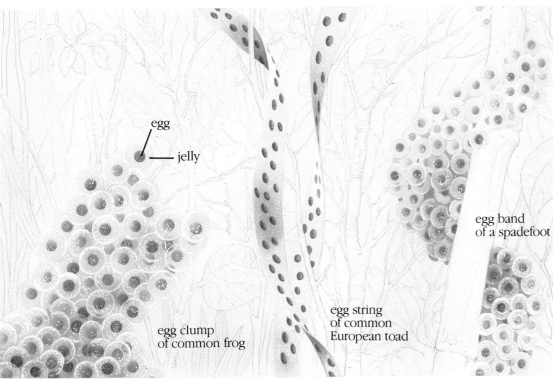

egg
— jelly

egg clump
of common frog

egg string
of common
European toad

egg band
of a spadefoot

Left: the amphibians' eggs, particularly those of the anurans, are laid in water, enveloped in a gelatinous substance. They are laid on the bottom or left hanging from aquatic plants.

Above: a few anuran species lay eggs from which perfectly formed young hatch. Here we see the eggs of a South African *Breviceps adspersus*.

adult

specimen with
four limbs
and atrophied tail

tadpole with internal
gills and hindleg
already formed

Crested newt

male

female

egg

In the mating season, the male crested newt, a urodele amphibian common in Europe, has a conspicuous toothed crest on its back. The creature performs an established ritual with complicated movements to seduce the female without ever touching her. The female, less showy than the male, lays each single egg on the leaf of a water plant in the pond where the ceremony takes place, and uses her hind legs to fold the edges of the leaf around the egg.

Midwife toad

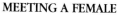

15. MATING AND PARENTAL CARE

From amphibians on, external fertilization—the laying of eggs and spermatozoa directly in the outside environment—which is successfully practiced by fish, becomes difficult. When water is scarce and space is restricted, this pattern of fertilization is too risky. On the other hand, amphibians have no copulatory organs—they will appear in the most evolved reptiles—and fertilization is therefore very complex.

THE MATING OF URODELES

It would be too long and boring to describe how every single species of urodele behaves during mating, but we can have a look at the behavior of the common crested newt. This creature can also reproduce in the laboratory, and it is therefore possible to study and examine it closely. During the

mating season, the male crested newt has a large crest running down his back, and is very brightly colored. Dressed up like this, he sets off in search of a female he can woo. But they do not mate at once. The male emits small packets of spermatozoids—called spermatophores—on plants; the female then comes along and picks them up, using her cloaca, and keeps them in her body. Fertilization is therefore internal, but the spermatozoids are laid outside. This seems to be an intermediate stage between the two reproduction patterns. This urodele female lays few eggs, and protects each one of them, placing them neatly in envelopes of folded leaves.

THE MATING OF ANURANS

As representative for this group, we have chosen the

common European toad, which can easily be observed during its mating routine. At the end of the cold season, the toads leave their dens, and wander around in search of a pond, a ditch, or any water pool for coupling must take place in the water. It is quite common to see groups of even hundreds of toads all traveling in the same direction. There must be something mysterious that drives them along in their search for water. It is hard to believe that these creatures, with their slow, goofy gait, can go a very long way, but they patiently overcome all obstacles and finally reach their destination.

MEETING A FEMALE

There is no balance between male and female toads, for the former largely outnumber the latter—many

Surinam toad

Phyllobates bicolor

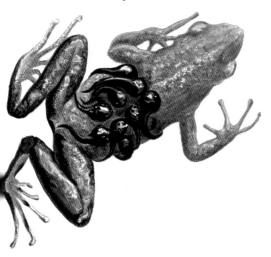

Common European toad

Left, top: the female Surinam toad, one of the few anuran amphibians that look after their young, protects the eggs by keeping them in special little chambers in the spongy skin of her back. The male midwife toad keeps the eggs in incubation, winding the egg string around his hindlegs. The male *Phyllobates bicolor* carries the tadpoles on his back.

Anuran amphibians always mate in the water, and their way of mating is very different from that of the urodeles. Without any preliminaries, the male clasps the female and fertilizes the eggs that she lays. We can see here a pair of common European toads still clasping after the mating, which lasted many hours, among the water plants to which the egg bands are attached.

male toads will have made the long trip in vain. The meeting of the two sexes is casual, for there is no courtship. When a male has approached a female, it is soon clinging very closely to her back, and will not move until coupling is over. If another male wants to climb on the female's back, a kind of fight takes place between the two kicking toads; but usually, the first toad never lets go. Often, a whole group of males try to cling to one and the same female, and if she is much larger than the males—as often happens—there can be two rivals on her back at the same time.

THE MALE'S BLIND CLASP

The male's embrace is purely instictive, a typical nervous reflex. If you place a male on the back of your hand during the mating season, it will immediately take a firm grip on it, and you will be able to feel the toad's exceptional strength, belied by its moderate size. Its reaction is so blind that the toad clasps onto anything that might vaguely resemble a female's back. In the toads's mating season, it is quite common to see small fish jumping out of the water, trying to free themselves from the anurans' embrace; the scene is something like aquatic rodeo.

SPAWNING

Toads, like most anurans, spawn in water. Their eggs are protected by a gelatinous substance, and are abandoned, for immediately after mating has taken place, all the toads leave the water, and go back to their hunting patches.

PARENTAL CARE

There are rare examples of parents looking after their young. The male *Phyllobates bicolor* carries the tadpoles on its back until they are fully developed. The male midwife toad collects the eggs between his hind legs and carries them until they hatch, and the tadpoles are born. The female Surinam toad gathers the fertilized eggs on its back, where the skin grows, and ends up by enveloping them. So each egg is contained in a small cell, in which the tadpole carries out its development (see also Chapter 23).

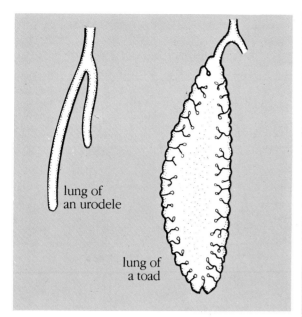

lung of
an urodele

lung of
a toad

The lungs of the urodele amphibians look like a sac with smooth walls, whereas those of the anurans are rougher.

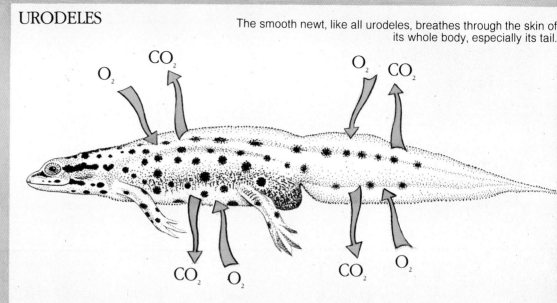

The smooth newt, like all urodeles, breathes through the skin of its whole body, especially its tail.

O_2 CO_2

O_2 CO_2

CO_2 O_2

CO_2 O_2

In the larval stage, all amphibians breathe through gills, which are at first external, and then become internal. Here, we see the larva of a smooth newt.

16. RESPIRATION, VOICE, AND BLOOD

HOW THEY BREATHE

We already know that lungs were invented by sarcopterygian fish, but they only used them either to augment the gills, or to enable the creatures to survive during periods of drought. In amphibians, on the contrary, the task of the lungs is to satisfy the creature's need for oxygen. Their structure is still primitive, and not very functional: they are merely empty sacs, with almost smooth walls. Lungs like these were not able to meet all the animal's oxygen requirements, so the amphibians developed other ways of breathing.

THE RESPIRATION OF URODELES

These animals solve the problem by using their tails—which are very wide and rich in blood vessels—to facilitate the interchange of respiratory gases. The blood takes in oxygen and releases carbon dioxide. The whole skin surface accomplishes the same task so that the lung is not really so important. Indeed, there are certain urodeles with an atrophied—and therefore useless—lung. They ignore the air altogether, and take their oxygen exclusively from the water.

THE RESPIRATION OF ANURANS

This amphibian has a higher rate of metabolism than urodeles do, and its need for oxygen is therefore greater. It does have a lung, but not a very efficient one. The anuran has no tail to help oxygenate its blood, so the function is carried out by the lung, the skin, and mostly, by the mouth. The inner walls of its enormous mouth are extremely rich in blood vessels,

and most of the anuran's respiration occurs here. The oxygen in the air (O_2) dissolves in the moisture which dampens the inner walls of the mouth, through which it flows on its way to the blood. The reverse occurs for carbon dioxide (CO_2). The respiration system of these amphibians is very simple. The anuran removes air from its oral cavity by lowering and raising the floor of its mouth. If you look at a frog's throat, you will notice that it never stops vibrating as it expels air through its nostrils and breathes fresh air in. Air is pushed into the lungs little by little, as if the frog were sipping it. Then, inside the lungs, the interchange of respiratory gases takes place. It sometimes takes as much as several minutes before the air has been changed completely.

THE VOICE OF AMPHIBIANS

When amphibians decided to leave the water, the air was already ringing with crying and singing. Invertebrates, in fact, had abandoned the water many millions of years earlier, and had invented calls to express appeal, challenge, and dominion. With the amphibians, another stronger and harsher voice came in. While the urodeles remained dumb, the anurans—

METABOLISM

The reactions that take place in the cells of an organism can be more or less rapid, depending on the hormones in the thyroid gland. An animal with a high rate of metabolism reacts more rapidly, moves more quickly, and responds more promptly to environmental stimuli, while an animal with a low rate metabolism moves lazily, and its reactions are slow. One of the consequences of the different metabolisms is the variable consumption of oxygen. The higher the rate of metabolism, the more oxygen is needed by cells, and vice versa.

Anurans breathe both through the lungs and through the mucous membrane of the mouth.
The bottom of the mouth is covered by the mylohyoid muscle, which moves downward, thus expanding the oral cavity and letting the oxygen (O_2) in through the nostrils.

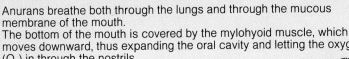

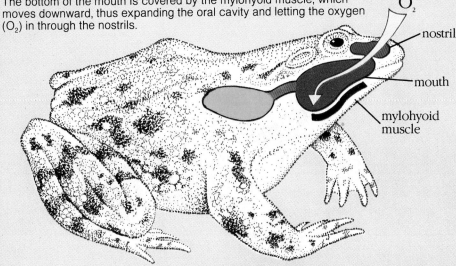

O_2

nostril

mouth

mylohyoid muscle

The edible frog has two vocal sacs at the sides of its mouth.

CO_2

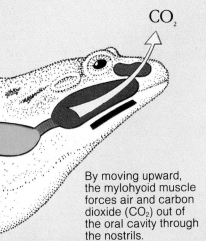

By moving upward, the mylohyoid muscle forces air and carbon dioxide (CO_2) out of the oral cavity through the nostrils.

The European tree frog (above) and the marine toad (left) have a vocal sac at the bottom of their mouths.

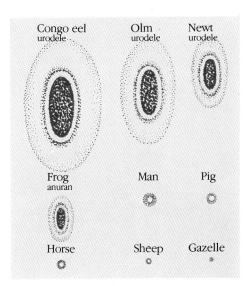

Congo eel urodele	Olm urodele	Newt urodele
Frog anuran	Man	Pig
Horse	Sheep	Gazelle

The red cells of the amphibians set a record, as far as their size is concerned: the largest ones are those of the urodeles; they are evidence of the slow metabolism of these creatures.

Above and left: in many male anurans, the croak produced by the vocal cords is greatly amplified through the vocal sac, a sound box made of very elastic, wrinkly skin, which swells like a balloon when the air passes through it.

but only the males—developed an extraordinarily wide variety of sounds, with some very high, fairly loud tones. The bullfrog (see also Chapters 17 and 25) emits the most peculiar sound for an amphibian: it moos—whence its name—instead of croaking. If you hear it singing in the dark of the night, your blood may well run cold, for it sounds like the cry of a some mysterious, invisible wild animal. But, generally speaking, the anuran's singing is softer and more characteristic; it is produced by two swelling vocal sacs on both sides of the neck, or by only one sac under the mouth. These sacs can become highly inflated, as in the marine toad, or the European tree frog.

WHY DO THEY SING?

The question is simple, but the answer is not. Singing could be a sexual call, but anurans also sing out of the mating season. It could be a vocal means of saying "this is my territory, not yours"; it could be used for defense, but these amphibians are often so numerous, and so concentrated in small areas, that it

is difficult to distinguish their single signals amid the general noise. We shall be content with simply listening, for this is the first time we hear vertebrates singing, and it is a prelude to the splendid song of birds.

THE AMPHIBIAN'S BLOOD

This class of vertebrates has the lowest rate of metabolism. It is lower than that of reptiles and fish. Its need for oxygen is not very pressing, and the cells used to do the job—the red cells—are bulky and stumpy. In point of fact, the higher the rate of metabolism, the smaller the red cells; the more there are, the more oxygen they can carry.

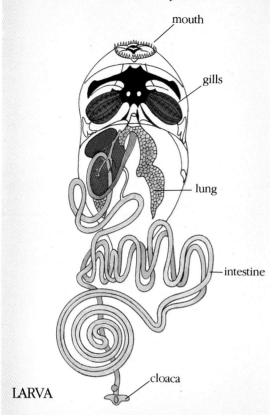

The intestine of an amphibian larva is very long, enabling it to digest the plants it scrapes from the soil with its numerous horny teeth.

mouth

gills

lung

intestine

cloaca

LARVA

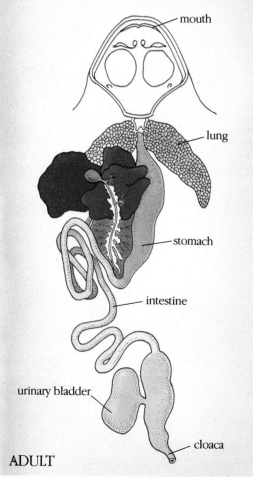

On metamorphosis, the intestine gets shorter, the small horny teeth disappear and the creature turns into a predator.

mouth

lung

stomach

intestine

urinary bladder

cloaca

ADULT

Urodeles usually feed on sluggish prey, such as earthworms, snails, insect larvae, fish eggs and tadpoles. Here we see a marbled salamander with an earthworm.

Marbled salamander

tongue

Head and mouth of a salamander.

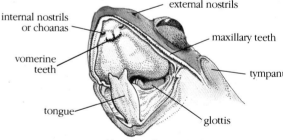

external nostrils

internal nostrils or choanas

maxillary teeth

vomerine teeth

tympanum

tongue

glottis

Head and mouth of a bullfrog.

17. HOW THEY FEED

WHAT LARVAE FEED ON

The diet of amphibians is totally different in the larval and the adult stages. The amphibian's larvae have little mouths with tiny, cylindrical, horny teeth they use to scrape and tear away the food, both flesh and vegetables. These larvae have an extremely versatile diet and are ready to eat anything. If they find the carcass of an animal, they are soon bustling around it, having their feast. But should no food be available, they make do with the green weeds covering underwater rocks in rivers. They have no competition, for no other animal can eat such a wide range of food, and obtain energy from practically every source available. This outstanding capacity is aided by a very long, winding intestine, which helps to digest foods of all kinds.

WHAT THE ADULTS EAT

Then, metamorphosis comes along, and the tadpole loses its fishlike features and aquires the characteristics of a terrestrial animal. Its diet changes radically, too. Its tiny, horny teeth fall out and its mouth becomes larger—even enormous, in anurans—and it usually, but not always, acquires teeth of the ordinary type. The intestine becomes much shorter, just like that of typical carnivorous animals. Adult amphibians, in fact, eat flesh, living prey, which they hunt skillfully. Their

Bullfrog

Hyperolius
viridiflavus

Anurans choose more agile prey,
which they catch in mid-air. On the
left, two bullfrogs chasing butterflies;
above *Hyperolius viridiflavus*, an
African frog, has just caught a
dragonfly.

Many anurans have long, sticky tongues that pop out
of their mouths to catch prey.

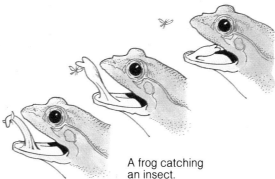

A frog catching
an insect.

diet does not include vegetables, only animals:
invertebrates, vertebrates, and small mammals, too.

HUNTING WITH THE TONGUE

While urodeles do not exhibit any special method of
hunting—they just approach their victim and pounce
on it with their mouths wide open—most anurans
have long tongues for catching their prey. This tongue
is unique among vertebrates, since it is embedded
just behind the mandibular edge and is folded
backward. When the anuran attacks, it opens its
mouth wide, and sticks out its long tongue, which a
gland secretion has made sticky. The movement is
extremely fast—about 15/100ths of a second—and

the prey is swept quickly back into the mouth. If you
happen to see a frog hunting an insect, your
impression will be that the insect suddenly disappears, so fast is the frog's tongue movement.

TEETH

Amphibian tadpoles have many teeth, but the same
cannot be said of the adults. Certain frogs have teeth
only in the upper jaw; toads have none at all. On the
other hand, teeth are not particularly useful to these
creatures, since amphibians do not chew. It will be a
long time before this important function appears. At
the moment, teeth are only used to hold the prey
firmly once it has been captured.

THE TASK OF EYES DURING HUNTING

The amphibian's eye has been closely studied to try to
understand the meaning of the messages it transmits
to the brain. In these animals, the sight organ does not
only receive pictures, which it then sends to the brain;
it also evaluates whether what it sees is possible prey
or not. First and foremost, the prey must be moving,
for if it does not the eye cannot see it; second, the prey
must have a particular shape. The toad's eye, for
instance, sends stimuli to the brain only if the moving
object is shaped like an earthworm; if it is square or
round, there is no reaction. The eye also estimates the
size of the moving object: if it is too small, no signal is
sent; if it is too large, warning signals are sent. So this is
an "intelligent" eye—it decides how to react before
the brain does.

THE GREAT FASTERS

Thanks to their low metabolic rate, amphibians are
excellent fasters during their hibernation/estivation
(see Chapter 19). Sometimes, months pass between
one meal and another, but the creature does not
suffer. It has been said that toads that have been
accidentally walled in have been found alive after
more than one year of total abstinence from food. The
only vital thing is humidity, for amphibians cannot
retain water; they must absorb it continuously, both
through feeding and through their ventral skin when
it lies on damp ground.

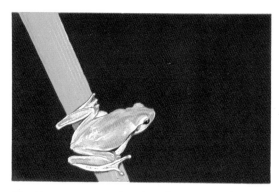

The European green tree frog lives among trees and the reed groves of the ponds, especially in France and Spain.
We see here this agile jumper caught in action.

18. HOW THEY MOVE

THE MOVEMENT OF URODELES

Many urodeles live in the water all the time. Some of them retain their gills even when they are grown up. So movement is ensured by the tail rather than by the limbs, which, however, are useful for locomotion on the seabed. But when the urodele leaves the water, how does it walk? Perhaps the rhipidistians had already solved the problem, but we have no evidence to prove it.

Perhaps the newts are the best walkers among the urodeles, but they still move in an awkward, goofy way. Three legs always touch the ground, while the fourth proceeds. Forward movement of the right hind leg is followed by the left foreleg, and so on. This gait gives an undulatory, snakelike movement to the head. In this case, the body is not lifted from the ground but crawls, and the legs turn into slim, useless stumps. These organs disappear altogether in the sirens (see Chapter 22), which have the typically elongated shape of species that crawl or swim with a serpentine movement of the spine.

THE MOVEMENT OF ANURANS

Moving toads are hilarious. Their stumpy bodies are lifted on their four legs, which move one after the other, in the same way as urodeles. In this animal, there is regression of a capacity which is, on the contrary, very common in anurans: jumping. The toad does not jump—or does it badly, the female especially—owing to its great size and stumpy body.

The hind legs of all anuran amphibians are suitable for leaping out of the water, and they provide forward thrust for swimming. The other classes—reptiles, birds, and mammals—also have tried to solve the problem of jumping, but the amphibian's accomplishment is second to none.

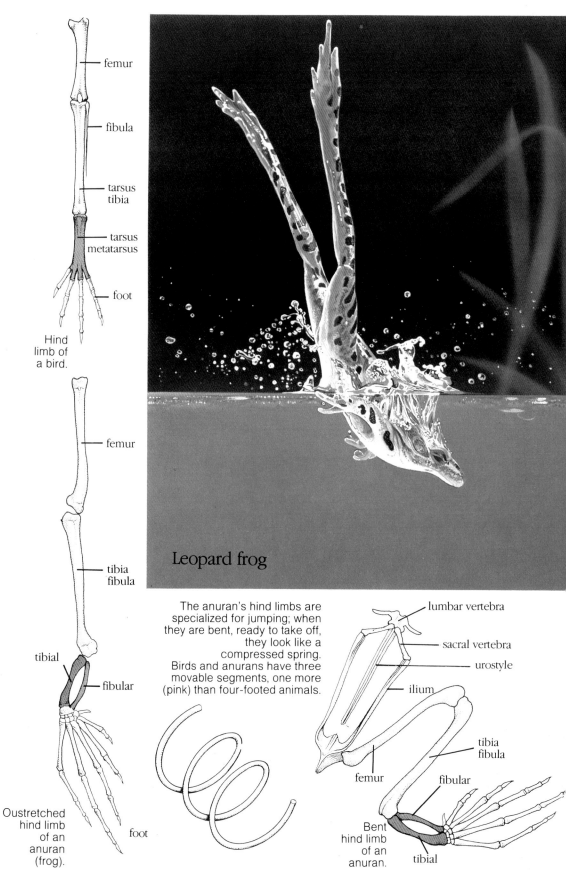

femur
fibula
tarsus
tibia
tarsus
metatarsus
foot

Hind limb of a bird.

femur
tibia
fibula
tibial
fibular
foot

Oustretched hind limb of an anuran (frog).

Leopard frog

The anuran's hind limbs are specialized for jumping; when they are bent, ready to take off, they look like a compressed spring. Birds and anurans have three movable segments, one more (pink) than four-footed animals.

lumbar vertebra
sacral vertebra
urostyle
ilium
tibia
fibula
fibular
femur
tibial
Bent hind limb of an anuran.

All anurans are powerful swimmers; one example is the leopard frog, the common frog of North America, which lives along the banks of ponds and streams, and, when it feels any danger approaching, it plunges headlong into the water, where it is better equipped to escape.

Phyllomedusa helenae

Some anurans and urodeles burrow into the ground. This is the underside of a common spadefoot's hind foot. We can see the typical "spade" on the first finger; it is a halfmoon of horny substance used for digging.

Other anurans, such as *Phyllomedusa* of South America, live on trees, and have hands and feet well adapted to a climbing existence; their fingers have adhesive discs which enable them to cling to the branches.

BUT THE AMPHIBIAN GOES FURTHER

That is not all. If you observe an amphibian's spine and pelvis, where the leg starts, you will be surprised to discover that the pelvis has a very long mobile bone, the ilium, articulated with the sacral vertebra, while the caudal vertebrae are fused, and form a kind of a bony stick, called the urostyle. Muscles for the long ilium and the other parts of the leg start from it. In our experience, we have never seen—nor shall we—that a part of the pelvis skeleton has lengthened and adopted the functions of the bony segment of the leg.

In short, these amphibians, ancient as they are, have managed to develop an extremely powerful and efficient hind limb for jumping.

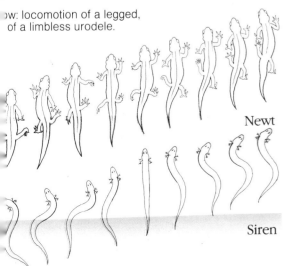

ow: locomotion of a legged, of a limbless urodele.

Newt

Siren

THE SPRING

In terms of dynamics, a jumping leg is like a compressed spring which suddenly goes off very powerfully. A frog's legs can be compared to springs with two coils, corresponding to the two mobile parts of the limb: the femur and the tibia-fibula, followed by the foot.

SIMILARITY BETWEEN BIRD AND ANURAN LIMBS

Very interestingly, this same avenue—adaptation of the leg to leaping—was also followed by reptiles, birds, and mammals. More particularly, the similarity between the leg of a bird and that of an anuran is simply astonishing. Both have three mobile segments, rather than the conventional two.

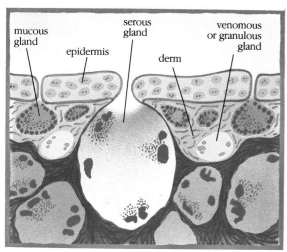

Section of the skin of a salamander, seen under the microscope.

mucous gland · epidermis · serous gland · derm · venomous or granulous gland

After sloughing, toads eat their skin.

19.
THE SKIN AND HIBERNATION

Poison-arrow frog

A poison-arrow frog with its two tadpoles clinging to its back. It wants to lay them down in their high cradle, a mushroom on the top of the branches of a tree, where the rain of the South American tropical forests has gathered; alas, the place is already occupied. This small brightly colored anuran is very poisonous: the Indians of the Amazon region use the toxic secretion of its skin to coat blowgun darts for potent hunting weapons.

THE SKIN

Before metamorphosis, a larva never leaves the water, and its skin is very similar to that of a fish, consisting of only a few living cells. After metamorphosis, the skin—especially in anurans—acquires new features: the number of cells increases, and its surface layers undergo partial hornification, becoming rich in keratin, a hard substance which protects the skin, and which will be used later in reptiles to form their scales. Some toads have cone-shaped protuberances on the skin of their backs, the warts, which are very much like a reptile's scales. The skin of amphibians, however, remains permeable; water, oxygen, and carbon dioxide can pass through it, and these creatures can breathe through their skin, too.

SLOUGHING

The presence of partially horny cells in the surface layer makes the skin very stiff and unable to grow as the animal does. If the amphibian is healthy and feeds regularly, its body becomes larger, its hornified skin becomes too small and must be changed. Sloughing enables the animal to change its skin and form a new, larger one, just as if it was changing its clothes. During sloughing, amphibians—especially toads—try to take off their clothes, scraping at them with their fore and hind legs. The skin comes off in strips, but it is difficult to be found because the toad swallows it up very quickly, for it does not want to waste the precious substances—such as proteins—contained in its skin.

THE SKIN'S GLANDS

The skin of amphibians is very rich in glands, which can be of two different kinds: mucous and granulous. The former glands are scattered all over the skin. Their task is to make it slithery, and protect it from

dehydration—that is, desiccation—when the animal lives out of water. The second kind, the granulous glands, produce various poisonous secretions in the different species of amphibians. These glands are usually found just behind the ear. They are called parotid glands—though they must not be mistaken for the similar glands found in man that produce saliva.

THE AMPHIBIANS' POISON

These venomous glands are a good means of defense for the species as a whole, but they do little to protect the individual creature. When an amphibian is being harassed, and even more when it is being swallowed by a predator, its granulous glands secrete their poison, which irritates the predator's mouth or stomach; the pain is so intense that the predator is forced to throw up the poor amphibian. So the predator, after a couple of unhappy gastronomic

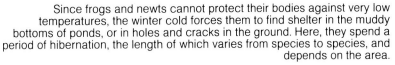

Colorado toad

Since frogs and newts cannot protect their bodies against very low temperatures, the winter cold forces them to find shelter in the muddy bottoms of ponds, or in holes and cracks in the ground. Here, they spend a period of hibernation, the length of which varies from species to species, and depends on the area.

Amphibians also fear lack of humidity in the air and very high temperatures. Dry heat makes the water in their tissues evaporate quickly; so they are forced to burrow into the ground, where they remain in a state of inactivity called estivation. This is very similar to hibernation: all the creature's internal activities—including heart-beat—slow down, and they survive on the supplies accumulated in their tissues, without eating.

experiences with these amphibians, learns to avoid them and delete them from its menus. Thus, the sacrifice of a few creatures ensures the survival of the whole species.

HIBERNATION

Amphibians are not thermoregulating, that is, they cannot keep their body temperature constant. When their environment becomes too cold, they are forced to hide away in sheltered places and reduce the rate of all their vital functions to a minimum in order to survive while waiting for better times. Hibernation, which permits animals to overcome bad times, will later be adopted by reptiles and mammals, too, with similar features.

For hibernation, toads find shelter in deep burrows they patiently dig. The amphibians that live mostly in water, such as frogs and newts, hide in the slimy bottom of their ponds. They burrow into the mud and

spend all of the winter there. They only breathe through their skin, for they never surface to breathe. During hibernation, their metabolism is so slow that their supplies of body fat and the oxygen in the water last long enough and are abundant enough to meet the animals' needs. Common European toads are actually said to be able to stay in hibernation for over three years, and then wake up from their long fast skinny, but alive—and kicking.

ESTIVATION

Some anuran amphibians live in very hot, dry areas. These conditions, just like the cold, do not allow the creatures to live in the open. They must rest in sheltered places, waiting for the climate to become cooler and wetter. Estivation is very similar to hibernation, the only difference being that the former protects from excessive heat, the latter from excessive cold.

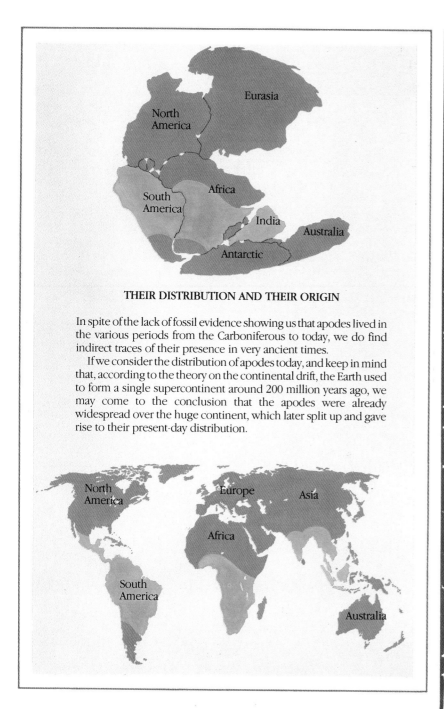

THEIR DISTRIBUTION AND THEIR ORIGIN

In spite of the lack of fossil evidence showing us that apodes lived in the various periods from the Carboniferous to today, we do find indirect traces of their presence in very ancient times.

If we consider the distribution of apodes today, and keep in mind that, according to the theory on the continental drift, the Earth used to form a single supercontinent around 200 million years ago, we may come to the conclusion that the apodes were already widespread over the huge continent, which later split up and gave rise to their present-day distribution.

20. APODES

We shall now examine the *Apoda*, or apodes—the word means "without limbs"—for they are the most mysterious and strange of the three amphibian subclasses. We do not know where they come from, who their ancestors were, or what their relationship was with the amphibians of the Carboniferous Period. Perhaps, their habits, or the tropical environment they lived in, made it difficult for their bodies to fossilize well. In any case, these amphibians provide a wonderful example of how a living form is modeled and adapted by evolution for life in burrows dug in the ground during the search for food.

THE APODE AND THE EARTHWORM

These creatures look very much like earthworms and they can easily be mistaken for them. They have cylinder-shaped bodies, with a series of ringlike folds in the skin, just like the large group of invertebrates, the annelids. The two groups are so similar, even an expert may be misled. Apodes can only be recognized as vertebrates by carefully observing them, especially their snakelike way of moving on the ground. In point of fact, no animal better deserves the name vertebrate than the apode, for it has more vertebrae than any other creature: always more than two hundred, and even three hundred in a species! Adaptation to life underground has not only caused the limbs and girdles to disappear; it has also made the body exceptionally long, and has endowed it with new vertebrae.

THE LONG-NECKED AMPHIBIANS

In all legged animals, the backbone vertebrae may be recognized because they have different features, depending on where they are positioned. There are vertebrae in the neck, in the thorax, in the lumbar and sacral regions, and lastly, in the tail. In apodes, as in snakes, all the vertebrae are alike. This makes it hard to understand where the elongation process took place, that is, in which area the number of vertebrae increased so much. But when we observe that the cloaca—the common opening for the rectum, and for genital and urinary products—is placed at the end of the body, and that the tail of all vertebrates begins behind the cloaca, we may conclude that apodes have no tail! If we then consider that the heart is very far away from the head, we deduce that the exceptional length of the body is mostly due to an increase in the number of vertebrae in the neck! If we added two pairs of legs to these limbless animals—and their ancient ancestors almost certainly had them—we would have an animal very similar to a giraffe, but with a long, wormlike body!

HOW THEY DEVELOP

Generally, apodes are oviparous, like all other amphibians, and they lay their eggs in water, or in

40

The female *Ichthyophis glutinosus* of Sri Lanka protects her eggs with her body, coiling around them and guarding them until they hatch.

If they had legs, apodes would almost certainly assume this position. That is why apodes are said to be the amphibian giraffes.

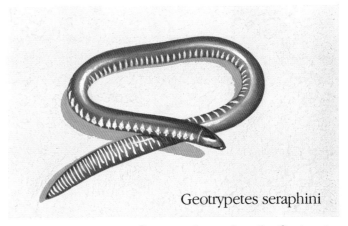

Geotrypetes seraphini

Some apodes, such as the *Geotrypetes seraphini*, are sometimes mistaken for snakes and considered poisonous, but they are absolutely harmless.

Environmental similarities, and the same way of burrowing in soft earth, determine a perfectly identical shape both in vertebrates and invertebrates. We see here a *Caecilia* gulping down an earthworm.

holes in the mud. The female *Ichthyophis glutinosus* coils herself around her eggs and protects them until the larvae hatch.

Typhlonectes, which never leaves the water, has an extremely advanced, sophisticated form of development: the eggs are kept in the mother's womb, where the larvae proceed with their development. During this period, the embryos feed on a substance called "uterine milk," produced by the walls of the womb, which are very rich in blood vessels. There is a very advanced, well developed nutritional relationship between mother and embryo.

HOW AND WHERE THEY LIVE

Our present-day apodes, which can be as long as four and a half feet (1.5 meters), live in wet or swampy areas in the tropical regions of Southeast Asia, Africa, and Central and South America, where they continuously dig burrows in search of food. They often plunder ants' and termites' nests. Sometimes, they leave their burrows at night to hunt in the open air. Their favorite prey are larval or adult invertebrates, but they do not disdain vertebrates, or even small snakes.

ADAPTATION TO BURROWING

It is certainly not quite correct to call apodes digging animals, since these amphibians have no organs suitable for digging. In actual fact, the creatures burrow into soft, muddy earth in the same way they move. Their cylinder-shaped, ringed bodies, and the hornified little scales on their skin, facilitate this peculiar way of living. Adaptation to this behavior has profoundly modified the general anatomical organization of these amphibians.

Not only have the limbs disappeared, but also the pectoral girdle and the pelvis. The eyes, being almost useless, are very small, atrophied, and often hidden under the skin; in one species, they are actually under the bones of the skull. The ears, too, have regressed, so that apodes may be regarded as blind and deaf. To make up for this, they have two small antennae near their nostrils, two tentacles rich in nerves, which are very sensitive tactile organs. These are probably the only really functional sense organs in apodes, the only ones that can help them to hunt their prey in the dark. But we know very little about the behavior of these creatures, which do not adapt to life in captivity very easily.

41

21. URODELES
*(Cryptobranchidae,
Ambystomidae, Proteidae)*

The order of *Urodela*, or urodeles—the word means "with tails"—includes specimens with long tails, small, not very functional limbs, and largely aquatic life-styles; some species never leave the water, not even for short walks. Cryptobranchids are considered to be the most primitive urodeles, and are common especially in Asia. Among them, the Japanese hellbender (*Andrias japonicus*) deserves special mention because, with its length of four and a half feet (1.5 meters), it is one of the largest amphibians living today.

NEOTENY

Neoteny (the prolongation of youth) is a strange phenomenon that occurs only in certain urodeles, mostly in ambystomids. It has to do with the thyroid gland not working properly, or with some dysfunction. The thyroid gland is the endocrine gland which, among other things, regulates metamorphosis in amphibians. The tiger salamander (*Ambystoma tigrinum*) was discovered during the last century, and it was believed for a long time that its larval form, the Axolotl, was a completely different species. In fact neoteny enables the animals to reach sexual maturity even before metamorphosis, so that they are able to reproduce during their larval stage. More particularly, the Axolotl can live, reproduce many times, and complete its life cycle without ever metamorphosing

Tiger salamander

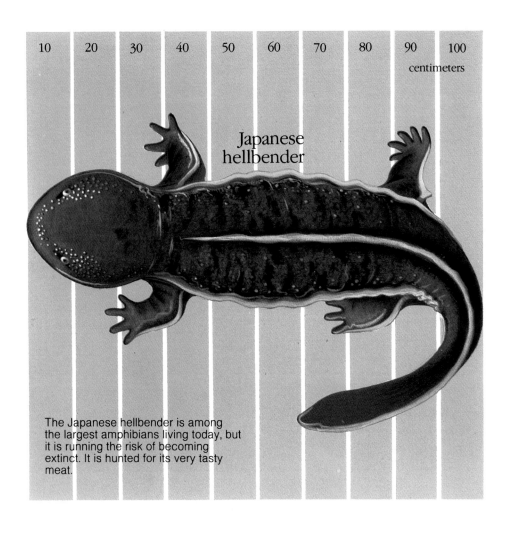

Japanese hellbender

The Japanese hellbender is among the largest amphibians living today, but it is running the risk of becoming extinct. It is hunted for its very tasty meat.

THEIR WAY OF LIVING

The way cryptobranchids live is quite monotonous, since they tend to remain motionless in their habitats for days, waiting for prey to chance along in front of them. Their very low metabolic rate makes these animals slow and torpid, but it also enables them to go without food for long periods. They do not need to bother much about the search for food. The large Japanese hellbender is very well protected nowadays, because it is running the risk of becoming extinct. Its tasty meat, and the possibility of obtaining certain popular medicines from its tissues, are the reasons why this animal is so actively hunted. It is also interesting to note that the creature is extremely easy to hunt, since it cannot defend itself, or get away, or even hide when danger approaches.

into an adult. So it was easy to assume that the Axolotl and the tiger salamander were two different species, two animals that had nothing in common but for the fact that they were both urodele amphibians. The connection between the two urodele forms became evident only when it was discovered that the metamorphosis process could be triggered off in an Axolotl by the injection of thyroid-gland extract.

THE AXOLOTL

This urodele amphibian has been and still is of interest, not only because it gives us an opportunity to investigate the connection between endocrine glands and metamorphosis—a process about which we still know relatively little—but also because its cells are very large, and therefore easy to study. Besides, the

THE THYROID GLAND

This is one of the oldest endocrine glands of the vertebrates, and all of them have it, even the most ancient. Its secretion, or hormone—the thyroxine—is accumulated inside special follicles, from which it is taken and put into circulation when necessary. The thyroid-gland hormone's task is complex, but it specially involves regulating metabolism, that is, the rate at which the various metabolic processes in all cells take place. In animals that go through metamorphosis, the thyroid gland starts the process and controls its rhythm, along with the sequence of modification.

The adult tiger salamander is 12 inches (30 centimeters) long and lives in the plains of North America. It plunges into the water only when mating. It can be developed in laboratories by giving food with thyroid-gland hormones to the Axolotl, its larval form. Its body is blackish, with yellowish speckles.

The Olm always remains in dark underground waterways, or in lakes in limestone caves on the coasts of Yugoslavia. It is neotenous and keeps its gills throughout its life.

Axolotl can be albino, that is, completely devoid of pigment, and it can transmit this feature genetically to its young.

ADAPTATION TO DARKNESS

Among urodele species, proteids have become adapted to living in dimly lit, or totally dark, environments. In such circumstances, specific features appear or disappear. The skin's pigment disappears, and the body becomes pinkish-yellow because of the red blood flowing in the vessels. And certain sense organs regress, such as, quite noticeably, the eyes. The regression of the eyes still leaves one question to be solved: why do eyes disappear when the animals live in complete darkness? Saying that it is because they are not used any more means applying

Axolotl

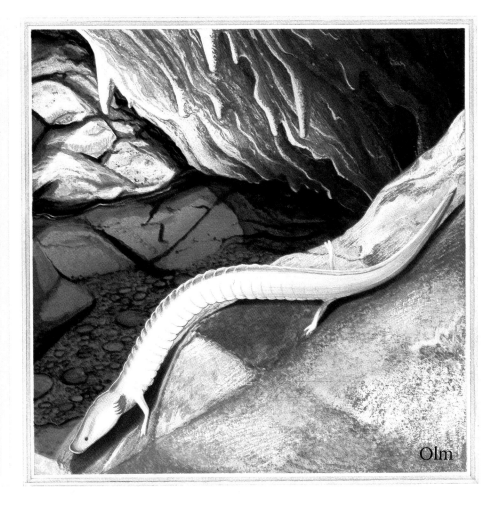

Olm

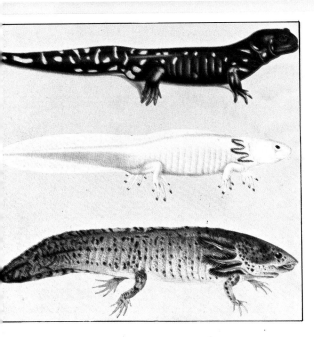

Above, center: Axolotl is the larval form of the tiger salamander. Like other urodele amphibians, it is neotenous; that is, it remains a larva throughout its life. It only lives in the Xochimilco lake, near Mexico City. It was known to the Aztecs (its name means "sea monster" in their language), who ate it, as the people of Mexico still do today. We see here an albino specimen of Axolotl.

A drawing made during a scientific expedition in 1882 shows the three forms of the tiger salamander. From the top: the adult, the albino neotenous form and the normal neotenous form.

Lamarck's old theory, which has always been regarded as wrong. But what other explanation could we give?

THE OLM

The Olm (*Proteus anguinus*), the most often studied species of cave-dwelling urodele amphibians, lives in underground karst (limestone cave) waters in Yugoslavia. Its long evolution, which took place in the dark, has made it totally blind. It has a typical white-greyish color, with bright red gills, but it is not albino because, if it is gradually exposed to light, its skin acquires a light brown color. It is clear that, although its eyes are atrophied, the creature—or its skin cells, rather—do perceive light rays and react to them.

In ancient times, salamanders were thought to be able to wander through fire with impunity.

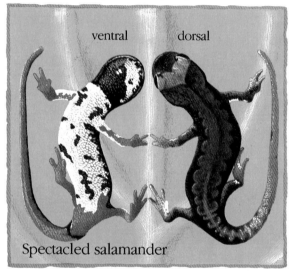

ventral   dorsal

Spectacled salamander

The spectacled salamander lives in Italy, along brooks in mountain woods. When it is annoyed, it turns and shows its belly to let other animals know it is poisonous.

22.
SALAMANDERS AND NEWTS
(Salamandridae, Amphiumidae, Sirenidae)

European fire salamander

The European fire salamander, which has terrestrial habits, cannot swim: when the female lays her eggs, she dips only her cloaca into the water.

Red-backed salamander

The Red-backed salamander is often bred because of its pleasant color.

SALAMANDERS

The salamander is probably the best known urodele amphibian. Pliny the Elder, the great Roman naturalist, mentioned it in his *Historia Naturalis*, and attributed to the harmless creature the power of putting fire out. The salamander, he reasoned, having the same nature as fire, must be capable of dominating it. This belief was passed on to the Arabs and to the Medieval European cultures, and it lasted until the last century. The salamander was believed to be the only animal capable of wandering through fire with impunity. It is hard for us today to understand how such a silly idea could have come into being and survived for so many centuries.

Unfortunately human credulousness has no limits,

is always ready to accept fantasy sooner than reality.

In actual fact, this animal has no magical powers at all. It is quite an ordinary urodele amphibian, widespread, especially in the Earth's Northern Hemisphere. Its most evident morphological features are the bright colors of its belly. The salamanders' coloring is quite unsuitable for camouflage, so the creatures are unable to hide safely in their environment; indeed, they sometimes do quite the contrary. Such is the case of the red-backed salamander, common in the United States. But there is a possible explanation for this phenomenon, which also occurs in anuran amphibians, as we will see later on.

When a salamander is in trouble, the glands of its skin produce a whitish secretion, which is definitely

toxic, and irritating for man, as well, if it comes int[o] contact with delicate, sensitive areas of the ski[n.] Salamanders are probably not a tasty food f[or] predators, so it is safer for them to be easi[ly] recognizable, so as not to be mistaken for prey. Th[e] salamander has no weapons for self-defense. All [it] needs to do is show its gaudy belly—probably to l[et] predators recognize it—because a predator that ha[s] already had an unpleasant gastronomical experienc[e] with a salamander will probably not be willing t[o] repeat it.

NEWTS

The genus *Triturus* is no less well known than th[e] salamander. In the Earth's Northern Hemispher[e]

44

The distribution of salamanders and newts.

Water snake

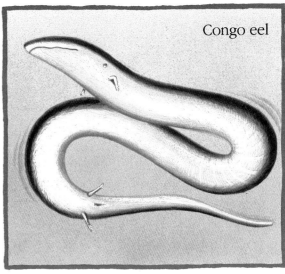

Congo eel

The limbs of some urodeles, which have adopted a snakelike way of moving, have changed in the course of time: they have become short, as in the Congo eel, or have disappeared, as in the *Pseudobranchus striatus*.

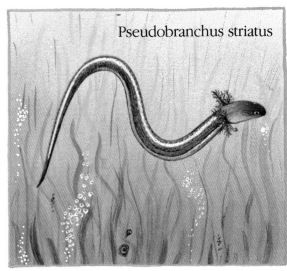

Pseudobranchus striatus

Left: the alpine newt is not only common on the Alps, but also in southern France, Yugoslavia, and Germany. It lives in sheets of water, where it is sometimes hunted by water snakes.

Alpine newt

newts are very common in all brooks, ponds, and very wet areas, and they are easily recognizable—particularly the males—because of the high crests on their backs. We have already pointed out that this ornament becomes more outstanding during the mating season, and it is quite useful for attracting females and convincing them to accept the males' spermatophores. The alpine newt is probably the amphibian that lives at the highest altitude, since it may be found at 10,000 feet (3,000 meters), thriving in habitats where even more advanced and specialized animals find life difficult. But this amphibian manages to carry out all its life processes, from mating to metamorphosis, during the few months when the temperature of the outside environment enables it to live a normal life.

THE DESIRE TO BECOME A SNAKE

We have already seen the apodes, limbless amphibians with cylinder-shaped, wormlike bodies perfectly adapted to crawling or burrowing into soft earth. The phenomenon is not an isolated one: in urodeles, as well, we see the tendency to assume a snakelike body and deprive the limbs of their original functions.

THE CONGO EEL

The Congo eel (*Amphiuma*) lives in the southeastern United States. It can reach a length of 3 feet (1 meter), and makes snakelike movements with its long body. It still has limbs, but they are reduced to useless stumps.

Perhaps they will disappear forever in a few million years' time. This amphibian's body becomes longer because the number of vertebrae in its trunk—and not in its neck, as happens with the apodes—increases, with the result that its fore and hind limbs are very far from each other.

THE SIRENS

These urodeles, too, live in the southern United States. They have cylinder-shaped bodies over 3 feet (1 meter) long. They are neotenous, that is—as we have already seen—they are able to reproduce when they are still at the larval stage. They have permanent feathery gills, typical of larvae, and too small to ensure good oxygenation of the blood; so, like all amphibians, sirens breathe through their epidermis. These urodeles have lost their hind legs and pelvic bones altogether, whereas their forelegs are very small indeed, and probably quite useless.

Surinam toad

African clawed to[ad]

One of the most bizarre-looking toads is the Surinam toad, which swims in the Orinoco and Amazon rivers. It has long, broadly webbed hind feet, and it is completely aquatic. That is why, like the African clawed toad and the yellow-bellied toad, it has the lateral line, a typical sense organ of fish. Here we see mating taking place.

23. ANURANS
(Pipidae, Discoglossidae, Pelobatidae)

The African clawed toad lives in rivers from Kenya to South Africa. If the water dries up during the summer, it burrows a hole in the slimy bottom, where it remains in estivation. It is very greedy and feeds on mosquito larvae, so it is useful in the fight against malaria.

Of the three orders of living amphibians, the *Anura*, or anurans—meaning "tailless"—are among the most advanced, and best suited for jumping, as we have seen. They are common in tropical areas all over the Earth and in other regions that are wet and damp. They usually live in water—frogs, for example—but some of them spend their lives in trees— rhacophorids—or on the ground—toads.

TONGUELESS ANURANS: THE *AGLOSSIDAE*

This suborder is considered to be the most primitive of the anurans, and it includes species which, although they have metamorphosed, and therefore lost their gills, never leave the water—they have become well adapted to this environment. The absence of tongues probably points to the very ancient origin of these anurans.

THE AFRICAN CLAWED TOAD

The female of this kind of anuran has been bred for analysis in research laboratories all over the world up to a few decades ago. It is extremely sensitive to progesterone, a hormone found in the urine of women from the first month of pregnancy on. So the creature was used for pregnancy tests. Injected samples of urine from pregnant women induced gravid females to lay their eggs 24 hours later. But after the test, the females had to be left at rest for some weeks before they could be used again. So the need arose for research laboratories to have hundreds of specimens ready for testing. Today, this amphibian is no longer used for this purpose, for it has been replaced by much quicker, and somewhat more reliable, chemical tests.

The African clawed toad (*Xenopus laevis*) owes its Latin name *laevis*, which means "smooth", to its extremely smooth, slithery skin, which makes it slippery and difficult to catch. Evidence of its great

adaptation to aquatic life is given by the lateral line which, as we already know, is a sense organ typical of fish, and of urodele amphibians, which never leave the water.

THE SURINAM TOAD

This anuran has no tongue, either. Its fame is due to the female's extraordinary habit of keeping her fertilized eggs on her back, enveloped by her skin (see Chapter 15). The Surinam toad is not a very pleasant sight. It lives in South American rivers, and never leaves the water. The mating ritual performed by this anuran is quite remarkable and complex, especially when the fertilized eggs are transferred from the female's cloaca to her back, for the male presses them into the female's spongy skin, which engulfs them. In a short time, all eggs disappear under the skin in special little pockets, where they go through their entire development, including metamorphosis. When the tadpoles have become

Yellow-bellied toad

Couch spadefoot toad

The fire-bellied and yellow-bellied toads are very common in almost all shallow rivers in Europe. Unlike the smooth-skinned African clawed toad, they have the very warty skin that is typical in toads. Above: a yellow-bellied toad showing its underside, in the threatening position it takes up when it senses danger.

Spadefoot toads, which live in the arid southwestern regions of the United States and in Mexico, avoid drying up by living underground. They dig shelters with the horny "spades" they have on their hind feet, and come out only at night, gathering around the few rainwater ponds.

adult toads—though still very tiny—they leave their shelters and start their own independent lives. During the first days, however, they do not stray too far from their mothers, but swim quietly near them, since they have no aggressive reactions. Cannibalism, a phenomenon quite widespread among amphibians, never occurs among the Surinam toads. There may be some exchange of signals between mothers and their young that prohibits such forms of behavior.

FIRE AND YELLOW-BELLIED TOADS

These toads do have tongues, although they still have the aquatic habits of tongueless anurans. They are well known for the colors of their bodies. Whereas their backs and sides have typical brownish camouflage colors, their bellies have gaudy yellow or red spots. These colors, too, are used for recognizability. When these amphibians are frightened, they not only produce large quantities of a toxic, very sour-smelling, secretion, which irritates the eyes and

the mucous membranes of the mouth and nose; they also take up a special position, as though they want to show their colors on purpose, as a warning to predators to keep clear.

DRY-CLIMATE TOADS

The couch spadefoot toad, an anuran that lives in the prairies of North America, gives us a good example of how it is possible to shape one's own habits and functions to the features of the environment. When it finally rains in those barren, dry regions, all the couch spadefoot toads leave their underground shelters and rush into the first water pools they come across, where they immediately mate and spawn. After only two days, tadpoles hatch from the eggs and start their swimming and eating. Metamorphosis, too, is gone through quite rapidly, and couch spadefoot toads can leave the water about twelve days after hatching, to look for safer shelter. A real competition takes place among the tadpoles, which must metamorphose

before their water pools dry up. Unfortunately, the competition sometimes has no winner because the water dries up before the twelfth day, and all the poor tadpoles die.

AN ATROCIOUS HABIT

Hammond spadefoot toads have adopted a very peculiar habit to speed up their metamorphosis. A certain number of tadpoles hatch and start eating algae and anything eatable they find, as usual. After a few days, some of them become cannibals and begin eating up their own brothers. These tadpoles, with a diet richer in proteins and precious substances, grow much more quickly and metamorphose much earlier than the ones that have kept to a herbivorous diet. So, once more, we see the survival of the species thanks to the sacrifice of some of its members.

TRUE TOADS
(Bufonidae)

The bufonids are another large family of anurans. They are also more commonly called toads. They are, in fact, the real toads, creatures that prefer to live out of the water. Like salamanders, toads are the leading characters in superstitious tales and beliefs. For instance, magic potions boiled up by witches often contain parts of toads' bodies, such as legs and skin. Many believe toads are poisonous, especially the urine they produce when they are taken in the hands. Toads actually are toxic, and one species, the giant toad, is lethal to man. But it is not their urine that is dangerous; it is the secretion of two large glands, the parotid glands. These are two egg-shaped protrusions that can easily be seen just behind the toads' ears, above the tympanic membranes—*parotid* means "behind the ear". Toads' urine, on the contrary, is absolutely harmless, and it is secreted because of a reflex very common in all animals—and in man, too—when the subject is very frightened.

TOADS DO NOT LIKE WATER

These amphibians look for water only when they want to reproduce. In the mating season, toads leave their safe holes and set out in search of a pond large and deep enough for them to meet their partners, mate, and spawn. Afterward, they leave the water and go back to their hunting grounds. During their migration, they often undertake long journeys, and have to face, and overcome, numerous natural obstacles. In the end, they usually manage to get back to their favorite habitats. This means they have quite a good sense of direction, but this aspect has never been studied in depth yet. Toads usually live hidden in damp and dark caves or holes, for they do not like light. They leave their dens only at night, provided that the air is not too dry. Their skin is not very well hornified—like that of all amphibians—and the creatures run the risk of dying of dehydration. This is why toads are usually seen more by night, when there is a high humidity level, or even better, after rainfall.

A PRECIOUS ANIMAL

Toads are fierce hunters of insects, larvae, and earthworms, and the largest species, such as the female common European toad (*Bufo bufo*), sometimes even attacks small rodents. In spite of these predatory habits, toads have absolutely no teeth, and have to gulp their prey down whole. Owing to their eating habits, toads are among the most useful animals to man: they cause neither direct nor indirect damage; on the contrary, they kill animals which are often, if not always, harmful. In spite of this, when a man sees a toad, the poor animal nearly always ends up worse off. Maybe it is the toad's ugliness. But is it really so ugly? Or is it the toad's undeserved reputation as a poisonous animal that tempts people to kill it on sight? In any case, killing a toad is very easy, for it moves slowly and is not such an accomplished jumper as its brother the frog.

A GIANT AMONG TOADS

The giant toad, also called marine toad, is common in Central and South America, and it is a real giant among bufonids, for it can reach a length of about 8 inches

(20 centimeters), not counting the legs. Its second name does not derive from any seafaring habits because all living amphibians dwell near fresh water; none of them, as far as we know, ever managed to reach the sea. The name "marine toad" derives from its habit of colonizing freshwater ponds, or rivers, but near the sea. It is very well-known because it often hunts insects in areas occupied by man, and it is not afraid of approaching houses and catching the insects that crowd around lights at night. But there is also a negative aspect in this toad's behavior, which may be the reason for its courage... or foolhardiness: its parotid gland can spurt a jet of poison up to 8 inches (20 centimeters) away, and since this substance is very toxic, and even poisonous if swallowed, all other animals have learned to keep well clear of this amphibian.

Toads live far from water, but in humid environments. They sometimes hunt little mice.

If a toad's tadpole is hurt or wounded, there is an escape reaction in the whole group.

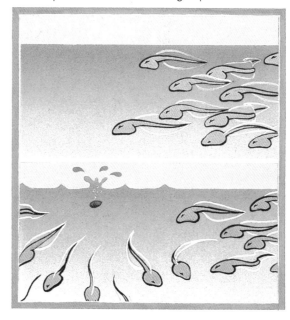

A TOAD FOR DRY REGIONS

Bufo regularis is common in Africa and Asia, where it has become adapted to life in arid areas on the edge of deserts. During the long dry periods, it remains hidden away in deep holes, which it leaves only during the rainy season to eat hastily and to mate.

A MYSTERIOUS MESSAGE

The toad's tadpoles have an astonishing behavioral habit that is very hard to understand. When hundreds of tadpoles hatch, and start grazing on algae, they usually prefer to stay or move all together, but if one of them is wounded, there is an escape warning that breaks the group up. It has been proven that the panic is not caused by any optic or acoustic signal, nor by vibrations caused during a fight. It is now believed that the tadpoles' skin contains a substance which, if released in the water when a member is hurt or wounded, causes an escape reaction. This is another means of protecting the species.

Common European toad

Giant toad

The giant toad weighs about 2 pounds (1 kilogram), and it is an insatiable insect eater.

The *Bufo regularis*, common in Africa, has also adapted to life in very arid environments; it hides in deep burrows during periods of drought.

Bufo regularis

25. FROGS
(Ranidae, Rhacophoridae)

The ranid family is distributed all over the Earth, wherever there is a pond, a river—though not a turbulent one—or even a high humidity rate. The climate they prefer is torrid, so large numbers of these anuran amphibians live in tropical areas.

THE EDIBLE FROG

The most common frog in Europe is the edible frog, which—as its name implies—has very delicate, tasty meat. These animals are, in fact, quite important because of their nutritional value, and this is why many farms have recently been set up to breed hybrids and obtain fatter and tastier specimens. These farms are profitable concerns, and since they are still in their early years, it is reasonable to foresee that, in the near future, it will be possible to breed frogs with large legs and small heads, as has already happened with other animals man has bred for his needs.

A SUCCESSFUL HYBRID

Zoologists today have conceived a theory according to which the edible frog is not a real species but a crossbreed of various species. According to them, this frog is incapable of reproducing, or at least not very good at it, and it is found in such a vast range of colors, it is impossible to define its typical features. But no matter how it developed, the edible frog is the most common anuran in Europe. On warm summer nights, the typical grating noise of crickets is drowned by its petulant croaking, which only stops if danger approaches. Its croaking is believed to be not only a mating call but also a challenge to rivals. If a male hears croaking, he immediately answers even more loudly. These frogs seem to challenge other noises as well, such as the rustling of leaves, or a train rattling by at a distance. The edible frog is particularly afraid of objects or living beings that move. If you walk up to a pond, there will be a general to-do among the frogs, and they will plunge into the water, but if you then stand perfectly still, the little creatures surface again, one by one, climb back onto the banks of the pool, and go on with their concert.

THE BULLFROG

The bullfrog is one of the largest anurans: its body alone is about 8 inches (20 centimeters) long. Its fame and name derive from the way it croaks: it sounds much more like a calf mooing than a frog croaking. Bullfrogs originally come from North America, where they are appreciated for their tasty meat and for their athletic ability. Long-jump competitions are organized for them.
Bullfrogs were brought to Europe by man, and live there mainly in rice fields. They even sometimes make headlines. If they arrive in a region where they were previously unknown, they may frighten the local inhabitants with their croaking—if we can call it that—and soon there is talk of ghosts, or strange phenomena, and the papers sometimes exaggerate the facts, looking for a sensation.

Bullfrog

The bullfrog lives in the United States, in the same habitats as the edible frog—though the latter is common in Europe. They are very tasty, and much appreciated by gourmets.

THE RHACOPHORIDS

There are many other kinds of frogs that deserve mention. Frogs are scattered over five continents and have the strangest, most diverse coloring, but a description of them all would take too long. But we may mention one frog family that left the water to colonize the treetops. They are the rhacophorids. These amphibians are especially common in Asia and Africa, and never leave tree branches, where they go through their entire life cycle. The ends of the rhacophorids' toes are fitted with small suckers, which they use to get a firm grip on the slippery leaves of those humid forests.

FLYING FROGS

Some rhacophorid species, such as Wallace's flying frog, have very long fingers and toes with a thin layer of skin between them. They spread their fingers and toes, using them to glide from branch to branch, and to brake and correct their direction. They do not have a true flapping flight, but leap from one tree to another, carefully controlling their descent with limb, toe, and finger movements. This is quite different from walking, crawling, or jumping, but true flight was only adopted later on, by pterosaurs—winged reptiles—which lived 150 million years ago. To complete their life cycle on trees, rhacophorids also have to reproduce among the branches, of course. They manage to do this thanks to the large amount of humidity in their habitats, and also thanks to the habit some species have of hanging their eggs onto the leaves, protecting them in an envelope of foam.

North America

South America

Distribution of the frogs shown in this plate.

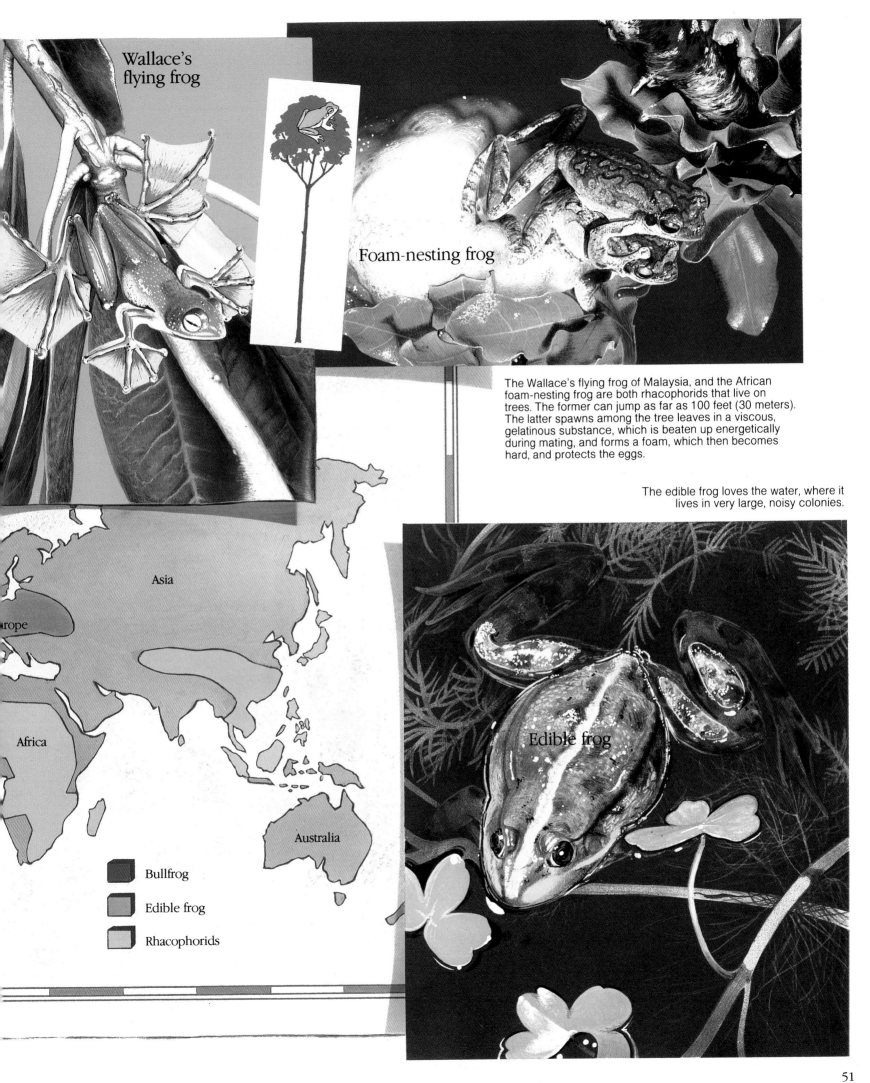

Wallace's
flying frog

Foam-nesting frog

The Wallace's flying frog of Malaysia, and the African foam-nesting frog are both rhacophorids that live on trees. The former can jump as far as 100 feet (30 meters). The latter spawns among the tree leaves in a viscous, gelatinous substance, which is beaten up energetically during mating, and forms a foam, which then becomes hard, and protects the eggs.

The edible frog loves the water, where it lives in very large, noisy colonies.

Asia

Europe

Africa

Australia

Edible frog

Bullfrog

Edible frog

Rhacophorids

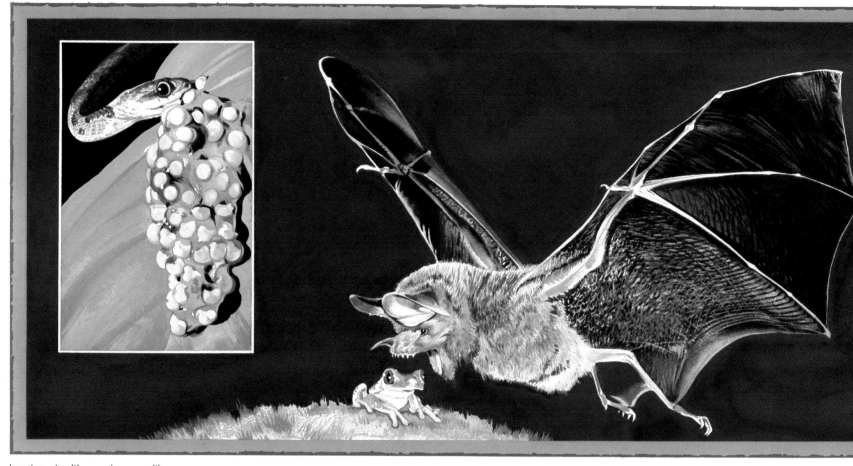

Inset: a stealthy snake greedily gulps down the eggs which a tropical frog has suspended from a leaf.

In the black of the night, a bat swoops down on a sr South American *Agalychnis*. On the upper lip of the there are "dermal denticles" (skin teeth), a sort of ra system that senses the frog's poison from a distance warns the bat of the p

Frogs can vary greatly in size: some of them are so small that we can easily mistake them for insects when they alight on flowers; others are very large, such as the African Goliath frog, up to 15 inches (40 centimeters) long.

Goliath frog

26. THE FROGS' NATURAL ENEMIES AND CAMOUFLAGE

THE PREDATORS OF EGGS AND LARVAE

Many animals have amphibians on their favorite menus. Their eggs and larvae are particularly appreciated.

Eggs and tadpoles have no particular means of defense: they are not toxic—unlike many adults—so they can be hunted by all sorts of animals, such as insects (dytiscids, dragonflies, water bugs), fish (carp, pike, trout), reptiles (water snakes, tortoises), birds

(storks, herons), and mammals (mice). And as if enemies from other classes were not enough, there are also amphibians that feed on other amphibians, such as toads, newts and frogs. There are also cases of cannibalism, as we have already seen: brothers devour one another; parents feed on their own larvae.

SAFETY IN NUMBERS

Such large-scale massacres could cause irreparable damage, even the extinction of the species. But in

nature, the relationship between predators and the prey is always well balanced; a certain number alway manage to survive up to the moment of reproductio Amphibians rely on the large numbers of eggs an tadpoles produced by each couple. In some case one female can lay up to 10,000 eggs; so predato have a great amount of food available. If only a doze specimens out of the 10,000 manage to becom sexually mature and reproduce, that is still quit enough to ensure the survival of the species.

To show the great variety of skin colors of these anurans, and their camouflage abilities, very different frogs are shown above. (1) *Centrolenella albomaculata*, common in the tropical forests of Central and South America. (2) The green tree frog of Florida. Its Latin name, *Hyla cinerea*, means "cindercolored", but this frog is a beautiful bright green. (3) *Dendrobates auratus*, very poisonous, is common in Central America. Although its light blue coloring is not very suitable for camouflage, the black spots on its body match its environment. (4) *Platymantis boulengeri*, from Borneo. Its shape and color make it look like a dry leaf. (5) The African *Megalixalus stuhlmanni*, cannot be distinguished from the rocks it lies on. (6) *Atelopus zeteki*, from Panama, broadcasts the fact that it is poisonous by showing its bright yellow color. (7) Albino tadpoles of the European common frog.

ENEMIES OF THE ADULTS

Adults can defend themselves more easily. We have already seen in Chapter 19 that some of them have skin glands that produce irritating secretions to discourage predators. Some species are hunted, because their meat is edible; their predators, besides the already mentioned animals, are foxes, hedgehogs, and even certain species of bats, which locate their prey by means of their sophisticated way of emitting sounds from nose or throat, and picking up the sound wave echoes with their large ear pavilions.

COLOR AS A MEANS OF DEFENSE

Like fish, amphibians, too, use color to camouflage themselves in their habitats. The colors of frogs are usually very bright and gaudy, and can change slowly, depending on the features of the environment. They do not have such rapid color changes as chameleons, but in frogs, too, pigment can move inside the cells, and affect pigmentation, adapting the animals' colors to the environment.

CAMOUFLAGE

Usually, the frogs' skin color mimics that of the environment, so that the shape of the creature is difficult to make out. Some species, though, have large black stripes to camouflage. Apparently, the general coloring of these animals is not mimetic, but when they are in their natural habitats, such as dimly lit undergrowth, with areas of shade and flashes of light, then their shapes seem to disappear; their outlines are lost in the environment, and the creatures become virtually invisible.

WARNING COLORATION

Toxic species have their skin secretion as a means of defense, so camouflage is not important for them; indeed, they need to be immediately recognizable. We have already seen that, in these cases, predators learn not to hunt poisonous species. To make it easier for predators to recognize them, their skin is very vividly and brightly colored, in contrast with the environment.

TRANSPARENT AND WHITE FROGS

Centrolenella albomaculata has quite an uncommon feature: it is almost colorless, and its small body is transparent, revealing all the internal organs.

Frogs, like other vertebrates, can be born without pigments, that is, albino. In this case, both tadpoles and adult specimens are quite white, and only the areas rich in blood vessels are a light pink. Albinism is caused by a mutation, that is, an error in the genetic code (see the volume in this series entitled *The Evolution of Life*), and the phenomenon is not really rare in nature. But white amphibians never live long because they are too visible, and therefore easily caught by their natural enemies. Nevertheless, if bred in captivity, they can reproduce and, in turn, give rise to other white specimens.

Cacops

27. THE DECLINE OF ANCIENT AMPHIBIANS

The dominion of amphibians lasted for the whole of the Carboniferous Period. So for over 60 million years, the Earth was inhabited only by amphibians, large and small, carnivorous and herbivorous, creeping and hopping. This was made possible by the climatic conditions of that period—stable, warm, and wet. Such an environment not only favored the development of huge forests, but it was also an ideal habitat for amphibians, which have never loved living too far away from water. And if the environment had remained the same, there is no reason why things should have changed much; the Earth would still be inhabited mostly by amphibians. But tragedy was already in the air.

CATASTROPHE

At the end of the Carboniferous Period, but even more at the beginning of the next period, the Permian— about 280 million years ago—the climate began to change. The humidity level decreased, the temperature started to fall, and the Earth began to feel the clutches of its first real glaciation. The climate

changed yet again toward the end of the Permian Period.

The air was still dry but the temperature rose, and a very long period of stable, dry, and hot climate began. Both events were deadly for the amphibians, of course, and in the Permian Period, the class began rapidly to decline. The orders became extinct one by one. Some of them, such as stereospondyls, found shelter in the few still hospitable oases and managed to survive until the Triassic Period, but their destiny was already decided—none of the amphibians that predominated in the Carboniferous Period has survived to our age. The true origins of living amphibians are still uncertain.

THE ROLE OF CATASTROPHES

What happened in the Permian Period may be regarded as a catastrophe on a global scale. In itself, it should be considered a negative event, but within the frame of the evolutionary process, catastrophes have a very precise constructive role. On one hand, sudden changes of climate cause forms that had adapted to

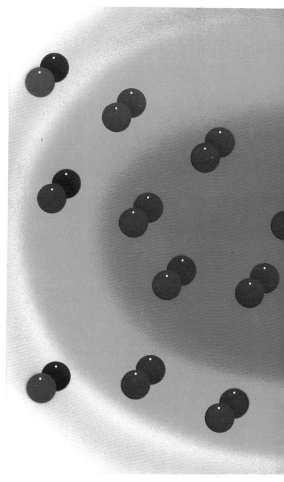

Eryops

The diagram illustrates a theory about the origin of the reptiles. In the central area, with a permanently damp and hot climate, there thrived those amphibians that had features typical of their class (the red dots); any mutation toward a reptilelike anatomical organization (the red and blue dots) was not welcome; so these creatures disappeared. In peripheral areas, where the unstable climate tended to become dry, those same mutations were so welcome that, at last, the reptiles appeared (the blue dots).

The Permian Period was characterized by a very variable climate: at the beginning, it was very cold (left-hand page); then, it became hot and dry (above). These different climates proved to be lethal for the ancient amphibians, which became extinct.

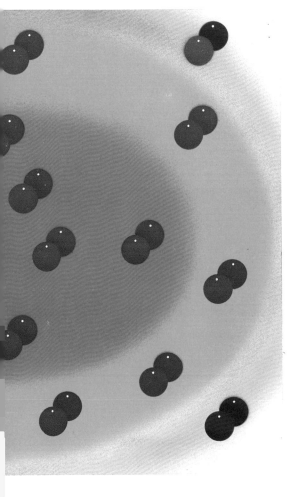

the previous climate to become extinct, but on the other hand, the same changes give way to other evolutionary lines in the areas now free from opponents. These new groups are better adapted to the new climatic conditions, and will spread and give rise to new living forms.

WHERE REPTILES APPEARED

At the end of the Carboniferous Period, when amphibians were still flourishing, the first reptiles were already on the scene. How, where, and why did they appear?

According to the first, and oldest, theory, reptilian features began to occur accidentally but progressively among the amphibians. These features did no good to the creatures, but they did not harm them, either. They were neutral, as it were. When the environment changed, the animals endowed with these new

characteristics were favored, and they asserted themselves. But this theory is in contrast with the banal observation that if a certain feature is not continuously favored, it soon disappears, as was the case with the eyes in cave-dwelling animals and the legs in crawling animals.

According to another theory—probably more realistic—although the climate in the Carboniferous Period was mostly warm and wet, there must have been areas on the edges of the land above sea level with a more unstable climate that tended to become dry or variable. Any mutations toward reptilian features that appeared in the central area of the environment more suitable for amphibians were not accepted by evolution, and disappeared, whereas if the same mutations occurred in the hot-dry peripheral areas, they could be favorably selected, giving the amphibians there the opportunity to move to drier areas and start to become reptiles.

28. AMPHIBIANS BECOME SIMILAR TO REPTILES

At the end of the Carboniferous Period, the reptiles made their first, awkward appearance. They were the forerunners of the protagonists of one of the most extraordinary and fascinating events in the history of vertebrates. Studies on the origins of reptiles aimed at establishing exactly which amphibians were their ancestors have provided no certain data yet, only rough hints.

THE *SEYMOURIA*, THE MAJOR CANDIDATE

In the Carboniferous and Permian Periods, the seymouriamorphs, amphibians of rather modest size, were quite widespread. They were no more than 3 feet (1 meter) long, and had a shape similar to that of lizards. One of them, *Seymouria*, has been very carefully studied, since it had certain unique features for an amphibian of that period. First of all, the creature was definitely an amphibian, since it had to go through metamorphosis to become an adult. At the same time, however, it also had reptilelike skeletal features, together with the more typically amphibian ones, and even fishlike ones. In such—not very frequent—cases, paleontologists speak of "mosaic" evolution because of the variety of different features in one and the same animal. *Seymouria* is actually made up like a mosaic; it has 2 fish, 18 amphibian, and as many as 11 reptilian features.

IS *SEYMOURIA* STILL AN AMPHIBIAN?

This amphibian's reptilelike features have led many scholars to regard it as a forerunner of the reptiles. But a more careful and recent enquiry excludes this theory. *Seymouria* was flourishing when reptiles had already appeared, so it cannot have been this amphibian that turned into a reptile. Besides, examination of its skull reveals that it still had a lateral line, which, as we have seen in another volume of this series, *Marine Life*, is a typical sense organ of animals living in water, that is, in a habitat unsuitable for the evolution of reptiles.

THE PROTAGONIST IS STILL UNKNOWN

Now that the hypothesis of *Seymouria* as an almost reptile, or something on its way to becoming one, has been rejected, studies are being made to find the leading character in the transition toward the new class, but nothing new has emerged to date. *Seymouria* belongs to the larger group, or suborder, of seymouriamorphs, one of which may have left the water and set off in a new evolutionary direction, acquiring the specific features of terrestrial animals like reptiles.

THE FIRST REPTILES

The oldest reptiles, dating back to the Carboniferous Period—around 300 million years ago—are called cotylosaurs. Their body shapes, still heavy, were similar to those of the amphibians; only the limbs were stumpier and more powerful. But their way of walking was still slow, and their spinal column bent from right to left, with the typical swaying movement of urodeles. These first reptiles were not very large, and they had no precise specialization, which supports the observation that only generical organisms are flexible enough to trigger off great changes.

THE CREATIVE CATASTROPHE

Observing these animals, the validity of the statement on the constructive capacity of catastrophes we made in Chapter 27 is borne out. Because of their moderate size and restricted specialization, these first reptiles were certainly not able to compete with the amphibians nor chase them from their habitats. The amphibians that lived in the late Carboniferous Period were already too advanced, too specialized and well adapted to the environment, to let these scarcely competitive reptilelike creatures oust them. Only by the sacrifice of amphibians—owing to sudden climatic changes—did the cotylosaurs have a chance of making their presence felt, and they spread, giving rise to the large, rather fortunate class of reptiles.

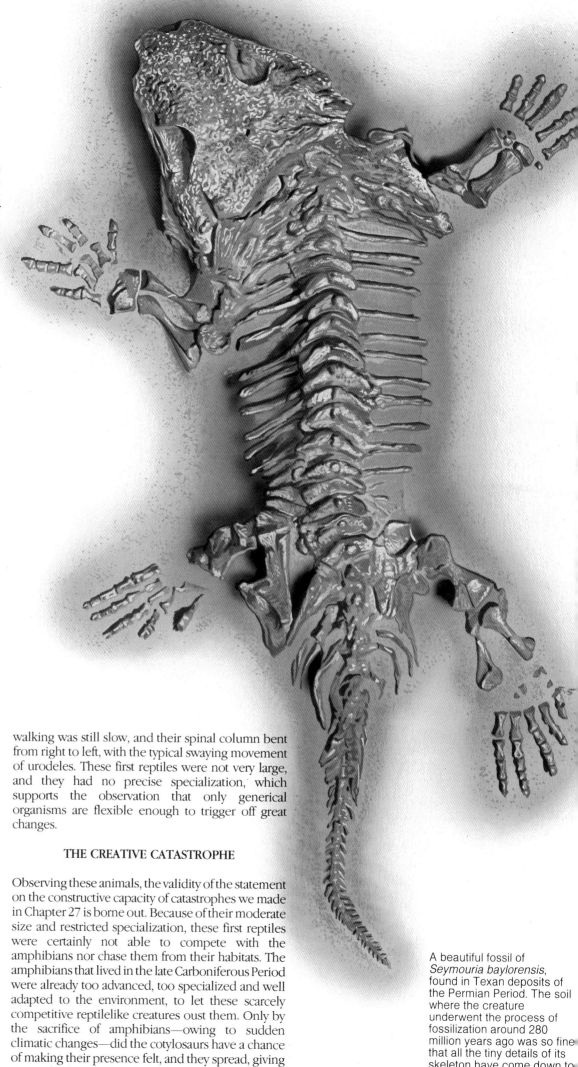

A beautiful fossil of *Seymouria baylorensis*, found in Texan deposits of the Permian Period. The soil where the creature underwent the process of fossilization around 280 million years ago was so fine that all the tiny details of its skeleton have come down to us in perfect condition.

Much painstaking work is needed to unearth the fossil remains of prehistoric animals. Every care has to be taken to avoid causing damage to the precious specimens that the rock has kept for us for so many million years.

RECONSTRUCTIONS

When we find the skeleton of an animal that is extinct today, and we want to get to know it a little better, we reconstruct it, covering its bones with muscles and skin. This task is not entrusted only to the hands and imagination of the researchers. When fitted to a piece of bone, muscles tend to leave particular protuberances, tubercles, and crests, making it possible to establish the number of muscles present, and then to rationally recreate the creature. Of course, there always remains a certain degree of uncertainty, so that the reconstructions often reflect their author's ideas.
As in the case of *Seymouria*, the researchers thought it was almost a reptile, and so drew an animal very similar to a reptile, as we can see from the sketch above.

THE PROTAGONISTS' FEATURES

As we have already seen on other occasions, the protagonists of a great evolutionary transition, such as the transition from amphibians to reptiles, must have a fairly general, and not a highly specialized, anatomical organization. These are the fundamental conditions for retaining the evolutionary flexibility needed to carry out new adaptations. On the other hand, an organism that is specialized for a precise task proceeds along the same avenue and becomes more and more specialized. So it loses track of other evolutionary tendencies, and inevitably ends up face to face with its fatal predicament—when environmental conditions change and make its specializations not only useless but fatally harmful, too. Many of the amphibians of the Carboniferous Period could be accepted as candidates for the part of leading character in the great transition because they were usually not very specialized, and sometimes not specialized at all.

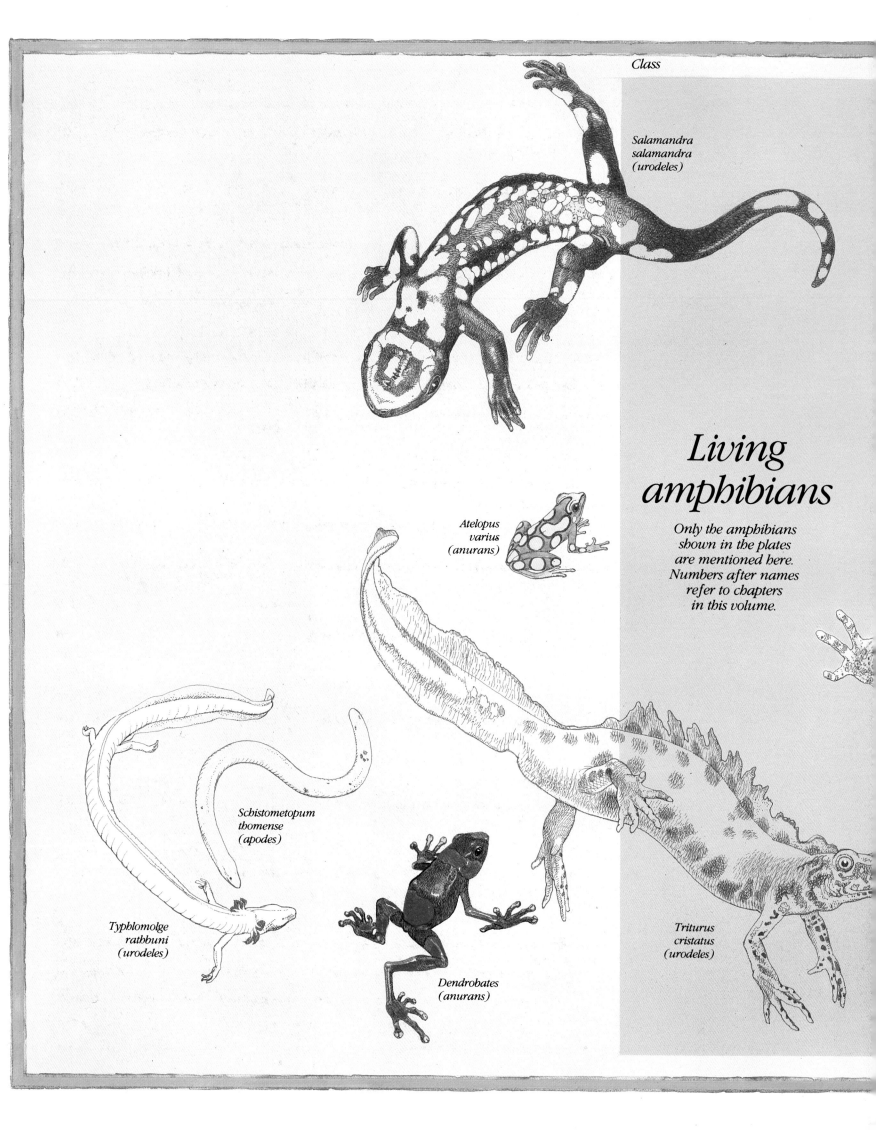

Salamandra
salamandra
(urodeles)

Living
amphibians

Only the amphibians
shown in the plates
are mentioned here.
Numbers after names
refer to chapters
in this volume.

Atelopus
varius
(anurans)

Schistometopum
thomense
(apodes)

Typhlomolge
rathbuni
(urodeles)

Dendrobates
(anurans)

Triturus
cristatus
(urodeles)